HISTORY

# THE SOUTH-EAST VIEW OF MANNORBEER-CASTLE, IN THE COUNTY OF PEMBROKE.

To Sr. ERASMUS PHILIPPS Bart. This Prospect is most gratefully Inscrib'd by his much Oblig'd and very humble Servants, Saml. & Nath. Buck.

THIS Castle is seated on St. Georges Channel, to ye South West of Tenby, and was built (as is generally Suppos'd) by ye Normans in ye time of K. Will. Rufus. It was held by ye Crown from ye time of K. Henry i. to ye Reign of K. James i. who by a Grant, which was afterwards confirm'd by his Son K. Charles i gave it to ye Bowens of Trelloyne, from whom it descended by Marriage to the Phillipps's of Picton Castle, and is now the Property of Sr. Erasmus Philipps Bart.

Saml. & Nath. Buck delin:et Sculp. Publish'd according to Act of Parliament April 5th 1740.

# MANORBIER PARISH

## *A History*

Gerald Codd

*Heliotrope Publishing*

Copyright © 2012 Gerald Codd


Published in 2012 by
Heliotrope Publishing
The Slough, Jameston, Pembrokeshire, SA70 7SR

ISBN 978-0-9523431-4-1

*Cover illustrations:*
*Front:* Aquatint of Manorbier by Samuel Prout, *c.*1810.
*Inside front:* Manorbier Parish from a map of Pembrokeshire by J. C. and I. C. Campbell, 1826.
*Inside rear:* Manorbier V.C. School, June 2012, on the occasion of Queen Elizabeth the Second's Diamond Jubilee.
*Rear, from the left:* Grove Cottage, Jameston; Lydstep House and Bay; Ashleigh House, Manorbier; The Laurels and Victorian Postbox, Manorbier Newton.

Printed and bound in Wales by
Dinefwr Press Ltd., Rawlings Road, Llandybie, Carmarthenshire, SA18 3YD

# CONTENTS

Acknowledgements . . . . . . . . . . . . . . . . . . . . . . . . . . .  6

Introduction . . . . . . . . . . . . . . . . . . . . . . . . . . . . . . . .  7

Prehistoric Manorbier . . . . . . . . . . . . . . . . . . . . . . . .  9

The Beginning of History . . . . . . . . . . . . . . . . . . . . . .  12

The Middle Ages . . . . . . . . . . . . . . . . . . . . . . . . . . . .  15

The de Barri Family Legacy in Manorbier . . . . . . . . . . . .  19

Gerald of Wales – the most famous son of Manorbier . . . .  22

Creation of the Villages, Manorbier, Jameston
    and Manorbier Newton . . . . . . . . . . . . . . . . . . . . . . .  24

The Church before the Reformation . . . . . . . . . . . . . . .  27

Absent Landlords . . . . . . . . . . . . . . . . . . . . . . . . . . . .  28

The Development of the Farms . . . . . . . . . . . . . . . . . . .  31

The Development of the Villages . . . . . . . . . . . . . . . . . .  37

Murder, Smuggling and Wrecking . . . . . . . . . . . . . . . . .  39

Religion, Church and Chapels . . . . . . . . . . . . . . . . . . . .  43

Education . . . . . . . . . . . . . . . . . . . . . . . . . . . . . . . . . .  49

Roads and Railways . . . . . . . . . . . . . . . . . . . . . . . . . . .  55

The Gentry and their Houses . . . . . . . . . . . . . . . . . . . .  57

The Entrepreneurs . . . . . . . . . . . . . . . . . . . . . . . . . . .  61

Farmers . . . . . . . . . . . . . . . . . . . . . . . . . . . . . . . . . . .  65

Houses . . . . . . . . . . . . . . . . . . . . . . . . . . . . . . . . . . . .  66

The Architect and the Parish Hall . . . . . . . . . . . . . . . . .  68

Poets and Writers . . . . . . . . . . . . . . . . . . . . . . . . . . . .  70

Memories (Hilda Hughes, Teddy Johns) . . . . . . . . . . . . .  71

Some Parish People (Builder, Blacksmiths, Post Offices
    and Postmen, Pubs and Publicans) . . . . . . . . . . . . . . .  74

The Parish Goes to War . . . . . . . . . . . . . . . . . . . . . . . .  78

Between the Wars . . . . . . . . . . . . . . . . . . . . . . . . . . . .  85

Change in the Parish . . . . . . . . . . . . . . . . . . . . . . . . . .  91

Military Manorbier and the Second World War . . . . . . . .  95

Fraternisation . . . . . . . . . . . . . . . . . . . . . . . . . . . . . . .  99

Evacuees . . . . . . . . . . . . . . . . . . . . . . . . . . . . . . . . . . .  102

Agriculture during the War . . . . . . . . . . . . . . . . . . . . . .  103

Tragedy of War . . . . . . . . . . . . . . . . . . . . . . . . . . . . . .  105

After the Second World War . . . . . . . . . . . . . . . . . . . . .  107

Parish People . . . . . . . . . . . . . . . . . . . . . . . . . . . . . . .  113

The Picton Estate Today . . . . . . . . . . . . . . . . . . . . . . . .  117

The Parish Today . . . . . . . . . . . . . . . . . . . . . . . . . . . . .  118

Bibliography . . . . . . . . . . . . . . . . . . . . . . . . . . . . . . . .  120

# ACKNOWLEDGEMENTS

To my invaluable typist, Brenda Cole, for her help and sense of humour, and to David Harvey for his help with research and publishing.

My thanks also go to Jean Kitchen and Dr. Wendy Raybould for their suggestions after reading the draft work, and to Tom Lloyd and Rob Scourfield for their encouragement.

Numerous people in the Parish, and outside, have helped with their memories and photographs, and I would particularly like to thank Gwen Rothwell, Molly Jones, June Stevenson, Anne Jewson, Dennis Williams, Dr. Ross Munro and Jean Kitchen. Also, Paul Curtis for his numerous loans of the Manorbier Census, Sue and Mack Robinson, her for her mother's memories and him for copying my fairly bad tape recordings, and Theo Parry for his drawings.

The staff at the British Library, Christ College Cambridge Library, the National Library of Wales, the National Museum of Wales, the Pembrokeshire Records Office and Reference Library and Tenby Museum Library have all been very helpful, and I thank them all.

Finally, to my wife Pam for her forbearance over the last four years on the topic of Manorbier Parish, and her recent invaluable help in making my work readable, and correcting my many errors.

Any mistakes remaining are mine and mine alone.

*Gerald Codd*

# INTRODUCTION

If you stand on Manorbier beach facing the sea, and then turn to the west you can follow the boundary of the Parish of St. James Church Manorbier which has been in existence for at least one thousand years. Manorbier Bay, carved out of Old Red Sandstone, is overlooked by an ancient cromlech, the Castle and Church. Walking westwards the next bay is Swanlake and the boundary goes inland halfway round West Moor cliff heading north. It goes west of Holly Lake, Slade Farmhouse and the village of Manorbier Newton. The boundary then turns east and follows the path of the Ridgeway for about three miles before turning south. Skirting the eastern boundary of the ancient estate of Norchard, it reaches the sea again halfway along Lydstep Haven. From the Haven, formed from Millstone Grit, the boundary follows the coast reaching the Limestone cliffs and caverns of Lydstep Point and Gorge. Then on to Skrinkle Bay where the Limestone abruptly changes to Old Red Sandstone. Walk on round Old Castle Head to Presipe Bay then to Priest's Nose and regain the beach in Manorbier Bay. The rocks you have traced on your way from west to east vary in age by an incredible 70 million years.

The Parish of St. James Manorbier has a total area of 5.87 square miles and a total population of around 1,330. There are four villages within the boundary with approximate populations of Manorbier with Skrinkle 645, Jameston 300, Manorbier Newton 50, and Lydstep 85. The rest of the population live in the scattered farmsteads (based on figures from 2001 Census).

What follows is a history of our unique Parish and its people.

# PREHISTORIC MANORBIER

Human occupation began in Manorbier Parish circa 10,000 B.C. About thirty flint working floors where flint tools were made and several hearths or burnt mounds for food preparation have been unearthed over the years. There would have been very few people living in the area, the population was nomadic and followed the herds of their prey.

Prehistoric evidence of life in the Parish was discovered in the early twentieth century on Lydstep beach. At low tide the remains of an ancient forest, which was submerged by a change in sea level, can sometimes be seen. The skeleton of a wild pig with a flint arrowhead in its ribs was discovered in the forest and has been dated to 5,300 years old. In Spring 2010 the tide revealed animal and human footprints preserved in the peat. The animals are thought to be deer and the footprints are mainly of children with a few adults. Perhaps the children were being taught how to become Stone Age hunters.

Over time the hunter gatherers began to develop a more sedentary way of life. Wandering stopped as people began to cultivate and harvest crops and look after their domesticated animals. This change within society allowed leaders to organise and create permanent structures. Kings Quoit overlooking Manorbier Bay is a typical example of a chambered tomb or cromlech (*Plate 1*). It is constructed out of the local Old Red Sandstone and has a row of eight large slabs which were placed above the tomb down to the edge of the cliff below. There may have been another tomb which has collapsed into the sea for you can see on the rocks below a stone which could have been a capstone. Such tombs were built for the elite, and although there is nothing to indicate who was once interred at such a magnificent spot, we can only imagine what ceremonies may have been held there by our ancestors.

In about 2500 B.C. stone circles and standing stones began to appear and, although the builders of Stonehenge used Bluestones from the Preseli Hills to the north, there are no surviving circles in the Manorbier area. Even so, the name Skrinkle may suggest that one still existed in Viking times, in Old Norse 'Kringla' is a circle according to the historian Edward Laws and Skrinkle may derive from this. The Parish did have a standing stone, described by the Ancient Monuments Commission in 1926 as being half a metre thick and standing to a height of 1.5 metres, on the Manorbier/Penally boundary in a field called Longstone Park. The stone has since disappeared.

The Bronze Age began in about 2000 B.C. and the Beaker people came to Britain bringing new skills with them. They buried their leaders in circular mounds called Barrows, with weapons and tools and small pottery vessels similar to a beaker, hence their name. These beakers are thought to have contained drink and food for the after life.

In Manorbier we have a rare group of barrows, one of only a handful of barrow cemeteries in Pembrokeshire. There are five of them at the eastern end of the Ridgeway and were intended to be seen from the valleys below. Unfortunately, they are not very visible now as they are behind the Pembrokeshire hedges on the Ridgeway. There is another pair at the western end of the Ridgeway with the Hodgeston Hill tumulus just inside the parish boundary, and the second one, Carew beacon, just outside. Some of the eastern ones were excavated in 1851 by a Mr. Dearden who first opened Norchard Beacon and found nothing. He then went on to another to the West and was stopped by an extremely large stone, weighing between three and four tons. Undeterred, our hero broke the stone by explosives. He found a skeleton underneath, and was disappointed that the skull was broken. Later on in the same year Rev. G. N. Smith did further excavations at the barrows and found Beaker pottery, one of which was a food vessel. This food vessel, which is about 6in. high, is now on display at Tenby Museum.

(By kind permission of Tenby Museum)

Rev. Smith also re-opened the barrow previously dynamited by Mr. Dearden and "felt convinced that a buried cromlech had been wantonly destroyed." No modern excavation has been done at any of the barrows and all that is left are some rather sad mounds in the fields. However, even now, centuries after they were built, standing on the top of Norchard Beacon, the view is amazing with a 360 degree sweep over the whole of the coastline and the Preseli mountains.

A late Bronze Age hoard (800 B.C.) has recently been discovered near Manorbier by a metal detector operator. There are nineteen bronze and copper artefacts with socketed axes, a fragment of a sword blade, a gouge, a dish headed pin and ingots and bronze casting by-products (*Plate 2*). It was found in an isolated pit with no evidence of settlement or a monument in the immediate vicinity.

The Iron Age, beginning in about 600 B.C., was a more war-like society. With the population continuing to increase the small amount of good land which was available became more desirable and each tribe built defences to protect their territory. The two major types of defences were individual defended farms and promontory forts. In our area there are cropmarks near to Manorbier Station which are identified as defended farmsteads and there are also two Promontory forts on the coast.

The first and largest is Old Castle Camp which has two embankments with ditches in front of each cutting off the promontory very successfully and two embankments protect the northern side. The Old Castle Camp is now inside the Artillery Range but it can be visited when the Army allows access. The earthworks have suffered over the years but there is a description given in 1871 of the camp before it was damaged by the military when there were rows of hut circles still visible.

The other promontory fort, Skomar Camp, is much smaller but is accessible with care. It is to the right of the Coastal Path between Skrinkle Head and Lydstep Caverns and is defended on three sides by cliffs, and the landward side by a ditch and bank. The present ditch is about ten foot deep with a similar height to the bank which would give attackers a climb of twenty foot to get in, probably with a palisade on top, so it would not have been easy to breach the defences. The inside of the fort is barren and rocky with no obvious sign of hut circles. Part of the defences guarding the fort have collapsed into the sea to give a perfect section through them showing the construction. This can be seen from the car parking area at Skrinkle Headland, overlooking Lydstep Caverns, just to the left of the concrete WWII observation post (*Plate 3*).

So, from the early, middle and late Stone Ages to the Bronze and Iron Ages, from hunter-gatherers, first farmers and early warriors, the Parish of Manorbier played a known part in all these developments of humankind.

# THE BEGINNING OF HISTORY

The Romans invaded Britain in AD 43 and the Roman occupation lasted until AD 410. For a long time it was believed that the Roman rule in South and West Wales only extended as far west as Carmarthen but recent archaeological work has indicated that Carmarthen was possibly the local *civitas* capital. Excavations have established the remains of a Roman road at Whitland with other traces leading towards Haverfordwest and probably as far as St. David's.

As yet, no Roman buildings have been found in Manorbier Parish but a Roman bronze/silver coloured trumpet brooch, probably used to fasten a cloak, was discovered near to Manorbier Newton.

Recently a group of five objects with at least three other fragments were found near Manorbier. The fragments are pieces of two dishes and a cauldron. The five items are a *trulleus* (saucepan) with a decorative plate on the base, two dippers and two strainers. The saucepan, strainers and dippers were found buried inside the cauldron. These would have been used for the preparation of wine, as Roman practice for wine drinking was to water it down, and sometimes to heat it and add spices. The owner would have been a high status person living around AD 100.

*Roman copper alloy vessels*
(By kind permission of the National Museum of Wales)

After the Roman legions withdrew in AD 410 there is little written evidence which survives for the early medieval period in Wales. Over time, existing leaders became kings who ruled their own areas independently. The historian Gildas, writing somewhere in Wales about AD 530, complains that although the religion was Christianity, the Kings "do not abide by its precept."

This is thought to be the period when the site of St. James Church in Manorbier started its life as a holy and sacred site. It may have been in use even earlier because there could have been a sacred spring on the site, as at Gumfreston, where people had worshipped. It is known that Christians sometimes took over earlier ritual sites.

The early Celtic Saints preached to their followers in the open air with the people standing like a modern audience in a semi-circle in front of the preacher. Early church enclosures are D-shaped to accommodate the congregation and later a covered structure would be built to protect the speaker, which then became the church itself. The site surrounding the church was the *llan*, a consecrated enclosure to bury the dead of the community. Our churchyard at St. James is D-shaped indicating that there was a Christian presence here before the Normans came.

The kingdom in the Pembrokeshire area was called Dyfed. It is reported by Asser, who had gone from St. Davids to be adviser to Alfred, King of England, that after Rhodri the Great had died, King Llywarch of Dyfed and other Welsh kings, asked Alfred for his patronage in the hope of assistance against the sons of Rhodri after his death. This plan did not succeed as Hywel the Good, King of Seisyllwg, grandson of Rhodri, took over Llywarch's kingdom and formed a new kingdom of Deheubarth in 902.

However, the request for patronage changed the politics of Wales for ever, as afterwards, the kings of England claimed overlordship of the whole of Wales. Deheubarth was split into *cantrefi*, one of these being *Penfro cantref*. This was further split into two *cwmwd*, and the eastern part of one is thought to have been Manorbier *cwmwd*. It has also been suggested that the beginning of the name Manorbier comes from the pre-conquest word *maenol*, which is a land division.

There are ancient field systems above Manorbier and Jameston villages which may be pre-Norman. The field system pattern has been fossilised by the hedges, and one goes north from Manorbier and stops about halfway to the Ridgeway, with the other going north from Jameston to the Ridgeway. A third field system is to the west and south of Manorbier Newton. Manorbier cuts slightly into the south-west corner of its fields, with Jameston village overlaying the fields.

These characteristics show that probably Manorbier, and definitely Jameston, had been built after the field system was laid out. The edges of the fields show the characteristic 'reversed S'-shape, the result of ploughing with teams of oxen. This co-axial field system has been dated on Dartmoor to the Bronze Age with the system continuing in use until 1000 AD as it was a useful way of organising the landscape. There are several co-axial field systems remaining in Pembrokeshire, some of which are definitely pre-Norman.

*Aerial view of Manorbier field system (1946)*

The use of the system in Manorbier Parish seems to have been to fairly share out the good and bad lands. With the field system running in a north-south direction, they go at right angles to the geological divisions between limestone, millstone grit and old red sandstone, so that the farmers had some of each type of land in their strips.

The Vikings raided the shores of Pembrokeshire from about 800 to 1000 AD. Some of them settled here and their influence can be appreciated in the many place names which have survived from Old Norse, such as Skrinkle, Skomar, the promontory fort on Skrinkle Head, Lydstep and Swanlake (Svanr Laekr = Sven's Stream).

# THE MIDDLE AGES

After the Norman Conquest of England, William the Conqueror visited St. Davids in 1081, either to pay his respects to the shrine of David or to display his power to the Welsh. He recognised Rhys ap Tewdwr as ruler of Deheubarth and for this privilege Rhys paid the English kings forty pounds a year. After Williams death in 1087, the Norman Barons were often asked to help in the wars of the Welsh. In 1088 Bernard de Neufmarché attacked Deheubarth. Rhys ap Tewdwr tried to resist but was killed in 1093. There was no longer any constraint upon the attacks of the Normans and a few months after Rhys's death, Roger, Earl of Shrewsbury, went through Powys and took Ceredigion, part of Deheubarth. His son, Arnulf, continued on and seized the *cantref* of Penfro where he built Pembroke Castle. One of the sons of Rhys ap Tewdwr was imprisoned by Arnulf and the other took refuge in Ireland. The chroniclers in Wales and England saw the killing of Rhys ap Tewdwr as the end of Kingship in Wales.

Arnulf installed Gerald de Windsor, maternal grandfather of Gerald de Barri, as Constable of Pembroke. During the Welsh counter-offensive in 1096, most of the Norman lands were lost and almost all of their castles destroyed but Gerald de Windsor held Pembroke against the Welsh. His grandson, Gerald de Barri, has a story of the siege where the Welsh were fooled into believing that Pembroke Castle had lots of provisions, and could withstand a siege, so they withdrew. After this, to try and keep the Welsh out of the Marcher Lordship of Pembroke, the Norman lords built a chain of castles and in doing so created 'Little England beyond Wales'.

When Henry I became King in 1100, Arnulf de Montgomery and his allies rebelled against him. Their defeat in 1102 meant that Pembroke March became a possession of the Crown, which in turn meant that the King had an interest in keeping the Welsh out of Pembroke.

A man called Odo becomes Sheriff of Pembroke around 1128 and it may be assumed that this is Odo de Barri. He almost certainly followed Arnulf de Montgomery and had been rewarded with an estate in Pembrokeshire. His son, William de Barri, married Angharad, the daughter of Gerald de Windsor, Constable of Pembroke Castle, and Princess Nest, the daughter of Rhys ap Tewdwr. Princess Nest, who was very beautiful, was known as the Helen of Wales. She had two husbands, and two lovers, one of whom was Henry I, and had children by all of them.

William de Barri made his first appearance in written records when he inherited the lands of his father, Odo, in 1130. It is recorded that he had paid £4 out of a sum of £10 owed to the King. Almost certainly these lands were the Barony of Manorbier. His youngest son, Gerald (Gerald of Wales), was born in Manorbier, and remembered playing on the beach with his elder brothers, Philip and Robert, who built sandcastles, whilst he built sand-churches. Some sources say that there was a half-brother, Walter, who was killed fighting the Welsh.

It is not known from where the de Barri family originated. The first Norman settlers came with a Christian name

*Gerald's grandmother, the beautiful Princess Nest – the 'Helen of Wales' – included Henry I among her many lovers*
(By permission of the British Library. Additional Ms. 10292, ft.21)

and a second name based on their village of origin. There is a village in Normandy near to Evreux called La Barre, and another village in Flanders near Tournai called Barry, so it is possible that a knight from one of these villages was in the original Norman invasion of 1066 and took part in the Battle of Hastings. A Guilleaume de Barri is on the roll at Battle Abbey, but this was devised sometime after the invasion and is generally now discredited. There is no mention of a de Barri in the Domesday Book so, if they came over with William, he did not think that their contribution needed rewarding with any lands.

Gerald de Barri, sometime after 1187, wrote that his family took their name from Barry Island near to Cardiff as they owned it and the neighbouring estates. There is another Barry island in the north of Pembrokeshire, near Porthgain, and some experts believe the name came from there. Unfortunately, there is no documentary proof of a de Barri connection to either place.

The fortunes of the family were changed in 1169 when Philip and Robert took part in the Norman invasion of Ireland, initially led by their uncle, Robert FitzStephen, but later under the command of Gilbert de Clare, Earl of Pembroke, known as Strongbow. Philip, who was now the eldest surviving son, was granted lands at Olethan in County Cork in 1183 by Robert FitzStephen, and founded the de Barri family in Ireland. Further lands in Ireland were granted to his son, William, so this became a more important lordship than Manorbier.

After Saladin took Jerusalem in 1187, the Pope called for a crusade to win the city back. In 1188 Gerald de Barri was chosen to accompany the Archbishop of Canterbury, Baldwin, to recruit for this, the third Crusade, in Wales. None of his family is recorded as going on crusade, probably as they were still consolidating their conquests in Ireland. Gerald himself set out on the Crusade but was turned back at Dover after the death of Henry II by the new King, Richard I (The Lionheart).

The descendants of Gerald's brother, Philip, continued as Lords of both Olethan and Manorbier. One of the more successful of these lords was David de Barri (1262-80), who became Chief Justice of Ireland in 1267 and a very wealthy man. He may have used his wealth to build the Chapel at Manorbier Castle, an ornate building constructed around that time.

Around 1300 John de Barri became Lord, and is first recorded in 1301 when he gifted the income of Manorbier Church to Monkton Priory. He had two brothers, David and Richard. David died before John's own death in 1324. Before his death, John had accepted a payment of £500 (worth about £250,000 now) from the Carews of Carew Castle, probably as an agreement that his brother Richard would inherit Manorbier after his marriage to a Carew. John may have promised both of his brothers the inheritance but, whatever he had done, there was confusion when he died.

After the death of John, his nephew David, son of the deceased David, moved into the Castle and assumed the Lordship. This infuriated his uncle Richard who, with the help of his in-laws the Carews, attacked Manorbier Castle, killing one of David's servants, and occupied it taking the £500 back from his nephew. It is not known when this attack occurred, but it was sometime before 1327, when Richard was thrown out by Roger Mortimer, Earl of March.

*Early fourteenth century effigy of a de Barri knight in Manorbier Church*

was pardoned by the King, Edward III, and he took over Manorbier, and left it to his daughter, Avice. She surprisingly left the manor to her cousin David's son, another David. This David, probably fed up with all the arguments, then sold it to the mistress of King Edward III, Alice Perrers and her husband, William de Windsor, sometime between 1362 and his death in 1392.

After almost 300 years, the de Barri's tenure as Barons of Manorbier came to an end. David de Barri, as lord of Fermoy, continued to be lord of the Irish lands, and the Irish lordship continued until 1824 when the earldom of Barrymore became extinct.

In St. James Church, Manorbier, there is a well preserved early fourteenth century effigy of a de Barri. In chain mail, with sword, and shield carved with the family arms the folds of the surcoat and spurs being well defined. The legs are crossed, and the feet rest on a lion. The crossed legs may signify that the knight had been on crusade. The identity of the person commemorated is not known, but the armour on the effigy is dated to about 1320. This would indicate that the figure is John de Barri.

David moved back to the castle and barony and Richard de Barri, together with his in-laws, the de Carews, was outlawed and became a fugitive. Somehow, perhaps after he was shown to be the rightful owner of the manor, Richard

# THE DE BARRI FAMILY LEGACY IN MANORBIER

The de Barri family built the largest and oldest buildings remaining in the village today, the Castle and the Church. The estate of Manorbier and Penally was granted to Odo de Barri sometime after 1093, when the Normans invaded. Although there has been a recent suggestion that an early form of castle, a motte, may have been constructed on the site of the existing Parish Hall, there is no evidence to support this theory. If it had existed, it would have been destroyed during the Welsh attacks in 1096. This may be why parts of the Castle we have today were built in stone at such an early date.

The square tower at the Castle gate, known as the Old Tower, was built around the early 1100's. The tower at St. James Church, and the old tower at Carew Castle are all thought to have been built by the same mason at about the same time. The Old Tower would have been linked to the contemporaneous stone Keep with a wooden palisade on an earth bank, which formed a defended inner Ward. Built not only for defence, the Keep provided the living quarters for the Baron and his family. Later, the wooden pallisade was rebuilt in stone to form the curtain wall and the entrance was strengthened with additional towers and a fighting gallery.

*Artist's impression of Manorbier Castle around 1300*

The Chapel was the next development, dated to around 1260. The finances of the de Barri's must have been good when they built this large, ornate family Chapel. It was constructed against the curtain wall, on an east-west axis, as was customary for religious buildings. The narrow gap between the Chapel and the Hall Keep was filled in with another three floored building. Under this was the passage-way to the Watergate. This range became the new living quarters for the Baron and his household. The curtain walls and the Old Tower were increased in height sometime later but unfortunately the extra weight caused the tower to collapse in later years.

Only one round tower partially survives with the founda-tion of a square tower of the Outer Ward but very little remains of the curtain wall of the Outer Ward and dating this has not been possible (*Plate 4*).

Nowadays, the Castle would have been in a much more ruinous condition had it not been for Mr. Joseph R. Cobb, a castle enthusiast. Born into a large land-owning family near Brecon he became a lawyer and made his fortune from railways. He leased Manorbier Castle in the 1880's and built a residence within the castle walls on the site of an old barn (*Plate 6*). He also rebuilt a lot of the walls, re-roofed the towers and installed new floors and fireplaces. Ground within the inner ward was cleared to make a tennis court and flower beds were planted. It is now a stunning holiday house. Mr. Cobb and his wife contributed to village life, and

held fêtes in the Castle, just as now. A bright spot of the school year was when they invited the schoolchildren to tea in the Castle.

*St. James the Great, Manorbier, circa 1900*

Manorbier Church's tower is built on the north side and at the west end of the existing chancel and may have been added to an earlier Celtic church. Gerald de Barri recalled hiding in the Church as a child during Welsh raids on Tenby. Originally not as high as nowadays, the tower would have served as a lookout for the Castle across the valley. The nave, north and south aisles, the stone chancel, and the transepts were all built as and when required and it is difficult to decide the sequence of construction. The bell chamber was added to the tower at a later date, probably to install a Sanctus bell. Professor Freeman, a Victorian expert on Pembrokeshire Churches, described the Church as "undoubtedly one of the most extraordinary edifices which it has been my good luck to examine, but really to describe either its outline, or its ground plan, is by no means an easy task."

The medieval estate of the de Barri's also boasted a fishpond, park and dovecote. Gerald de Barri writing in 1188 stressed the size and depth of Manorbier fishpond because they were expensive status symbols. The fresh water fish bred in the pond were used not only on meatless days but were a regular source of food. The Baron and his family ate coarse fish and his servants, saltwater fish. This is totally opposite to modern tastes, as coarse fish are considered far too muddy a taste. After Gerald's day, the fishpond at Manorbier was extended further up the valley, beyond the original small site under the castle walls and breeding ponds were added. In the late 1300's, carp were introduced via Flanders, and these fish, which were much faster growing, made fishponds a viable financial enterprise. The grant of Manorbier and Penally by Richard III in 1484 to Richard Williams includes the rights to 'stews, fisheries and stanks', a stew being a breeding pond for young fish, which confirms the extension of the original fishpond.

The Park is remembered in the name of Park Farm. The original Park was about 70 acres and was split into three fields, North Park, South Park and Garden Park in the 1500's. The Black Death, which came to Pembrokeshire in about 1348-49, reduced the population dramatically. All landowners had to devise new methods of using their lands, or they would have regressed to wilderness. One way was to create parks which were then banked and stocked with deer. Deer sometimes gave way to cattle or even horses, depending on which was the most profitable at the time.

Another source of food that began to be more exploited after the Black Death was the pigeon, and dovecotes began to be built, and the one adjacent to the Castle was built around this time (*Plate 10*).

The grant of Richard III also gives Richard Williams the rights to warrens within the Barony. At that time, rabbits were bred on a large scale for both their meat and fur. Conigar Pit, at one end of Presipe Bay, is the site of one old warren, as the name suggests.

# GERALD OF WALES – THE MOST FAMOUS
# SON OF MANORBIER

In 1188 the first written evidence for Manorbier comes from Gerald de Barri, the grandson of the first de Barri of Manorbier, Odo. Gerald is known by other names, Giraldus Cambrensis, Gerald of Wales, Archdeacon of St. Davids, Gerald the Marcher, Archdeacon of Brecon, and even Sylvester the Wildman.

In his manuscript *The Journey through Wales* an account of his journey in 1188 with Baldwin, the Archbishop of Canterbury, on a mission to encourage the men of Wales to take the Cross for the third crusade, he refers to himself throughout as Archdeacon of St. Davids. He was born around 1146 so he would have been in his forties at the time of the journey.

His life has been chronicled elsewhere, but his famous description of Manorbier is worth looking at here:

*"Only about three miles from Pembroke Castle is the fortified mansion known as Manorbier, that is the house of one Pyrrus. The same man owned Caldey Island, called by the Welsh Ynys Bŷr, which means the Island of Pyrrus. There the house stands, visible from afar because of its turrets and crenellations, on the top of a hill which is quite near the sea and which on the western side reaches as far as the harbour. To the north and north-west, just beneath the walls, there is an excellent fish-pond, well constructed and remarkable for its deep waters. On the same side there is a most attractive orchard, shut in between the fish-pond and a grove of trees, with a great crag of rock and hazel-nut trees which grow to a great height. At the east end of the fortified promontory, between the castle, if I may call it such, and the church, a stream of water which never fails winds its way along a valley, which is strewn with sand by the strong sea-winds. It runs down from a large lake, and there is a water-mill on its banks. To the west it is washed by a winding inlet of the Severn Sea which forms a bay quite near to the castle and yet which looks out towards the Irish Sea. If only the rocky headland to the south bent round northwards a little farther, it would make a harbour most convenient for shipping. Boats on their way to Ireland from almost any part of Britain scud by before the east wind, and from this vantage-point you can see them brave the ever-changing violence of the winds and the blind fury of the waters. This is a region rich in*

*wheat, with fish from the sea and plenty of wine for sale. What is more important than all the rest is that, from its nearness to Ireland, heaven's breath smells so wooingly there.*

*Of all the different parts of Wales, Dyfed, with its seven cantrefs, is at once the most beautiful and the most productive. Of all Dyfed, the province of Pembroke is the most attractive; and in all Pembroke the spot which I have just described is most assuredly without its equal. It follows that in all the broad lands of Wales Manorbier is the most pleasant place by far. You will not be surprised to hear me lavish such praise upon it, when I tell you that this is where my own family came from, this is where I myself was born. I can only ask you to forgive me."*

It is not often realised that Gerald is describing his birthplace from memory as he did not visit Manorbier during his journey. He starts remembering the landscape from the beach. After describing the Castle and its position, he appears to move his viewpoint to the Castle itself. From there, he moves in a clockwise direction beginning with the northern valley, moving on to the fishponds and moving uphill to the east to discuss the trees and crags of rock. Gerald then ignores the eastern side of the Castle and its principle approach route from the east, as well as the village. It would appear that he deliberately overlooks the working landscape of settlement and fields perhaps because it does not agree with his vision. He then concludes his description with the mill and fishpond.

There are some problems with Gerald's description, the most obvious being the position of the mill, which he puts in the valley near to Shute Cottage. The cottage has a barrel vault running along the length of the building and it may even be the remains of the mill, re-built later in the Victorian period (*Plate 18*). The mill could not have been in its present position on the fishpond dam when the fishpond was in use, so if Gerald is correct, something must have happened to cause the mill to be moved to its present position on the dam of the old fishpond. In a survey made in 1618 for James I, the valley between the Castle and Church was being filled with sand, making it almost impossible to keep the tail-race clear. The mill must have been rebuilt in the other valley using the old fishpond dam as foundation.

Gerald's comment about the Castle "if I may call it such" perhaps relates to his own experience of the large Norman castles that he has seen elsewhere in his travels in Wales, England and France. Manorbier in comparison, with its wooden pallisade connecting to the stone tower and keep, would have seemed very insignificant.

There has been a lot of comment about a vineyard, which was included in an earlier translation by Colt Hoare in 1806 of Gerald's medieval Latin original. This unfortunately rests on an error in transcription from the original manuscripts by a man called Powel in 1585. The incorrect transcription of the word 'vinario' which was translated correctly by Colt Hoare as vineyard, should have been the word 'vivario' which is translated as fishpond.

# THE CREATION OF THE VILLAGES – MANORBIER, JAMESTON AND MANORBIER NEWTON

When the Normans arrived in Pembrokeshire, their followers were rewarded with land which was taken from the local Welsh inhabitants. It was not just the Welsh lords who were dispossessed but also the people who worked the land. Manorbier, which was the first village to be established in the parish, was set out in a single planned row of plots on the right of the road leading to Skrinkle. Each plot or burgage consisted of one oxland of twelve customary acres (slightly bigger than the present statutory acre) attached to it within each of the town fields. It is thought that some of the burgages had two oxlands attached, presumably to reward the more important followers.

The earliest written reference for Manorbier is in 1146 by Gerald of Wales as his place of birth which, according to him, meant the house of Pyrrus. There is another reference written between 1136-54 in the Book of Llandaf where the village is called Mainaur Pir. This shows that the first element is based on the Welsh *maenor* and the second on a personal name, *Pir* or *Pyr*. Another possibility is that the second part of the name derived from the Old Norse *barr* which means barley.

Jameston village first appears in records as 'apud Sanctu Jacob' in 1295, and again as Seint Jameston, or Seint Jamyston in 1331, named for the Saint of the Parish Church. The village is different from the other villages in the parish, having a 'village green' in the centre but whether this is original, or the result of later development, is not known.

Manorbier Newton is first recorded as Neweton in 1331 and Neutoun in 1353, literally a 'new town' for Manorbier. Like Manorbier, it was laid out in a linear fashion.

Jameston and Manorbier Newton were established because the increase in population meant that more land needed to be cleared. The town fields of Manorbier could not be extended because the Norchard estate fields abutted them to the north and east and the Baron's fields were to the south and west.

There is disagreement on the order of the foundations of the villages. The argument for Jameston being the last of the villages to be founded is that neither the land nor the water supply was as good as the others, and thus would have been the last place to be settled. The argument for Manorbier Newton being the last village is two-fold. In 1293 David Martin, on his accession as Bishop of St. Davids, made an inventory of crops being grown in the villages of Pembrokeshire. Both Manorbier and Jameston are noted, but there is no entry for Manorbier Newton which implies that it did not exist at that date. The road which connects Manorbier Newton to Jameston, Haylands Lane, cuts across the Jameston village fields, so the road must be after the fields, again suggesting that Manorbier Newton post-dates Jameston.

According to the inventory of 1293, the crops grown were mainly wheat and barley with some oats, peas and beans. There were also cattle in the common fields. The method of farming for the tenants was that parts of the township fields were left fallow every year, with the remainder being cropped. They had their lands from the lord in varying forms and owed service to the lord depending on their tenancy. Each farmed their strips in the various parts of the fields when their labour was not required by the lord on his lands, the Demesne lands. In the Lord's Mead, just outside Manorbier Newton, after the lord had taken off the first crop of hay along Haylands Lane, certain tenants were allowed to take the second crop, which was a generous benefit as hay was essential to the survival of the cattle through the winter. There was also land owned by the Church and these are some of the fields south of the Church in the area known as the Glebe land.

The remains of a 13th or 14th century building in Lydstep known as the Palace has caused a lot of comment over the years. It comprises a first floor over three undercrofts with barrelled vaults. There may have been some later additions to the building which is recorded as abandoned in 1690. In the 19th century, one end of the Palace was being used as a cottage until it was finally abandoned in the mid 20th century. The Manorial Courts may have been held there during the Marcher lordships. The historian Edward Laws thought that

*The Palace, Lydstep.*

*The Place of Arms, Lydstep*

illustrated as here in his book *The History of Little England Beyond Wales* published in 1888.

The house was demolished in 1908, but a chimney and the remains of some walls can still be seen near to the Lydstep Tavern.

There are very few records for the arrival of the Black Death in Pembrokeshire. It seemed to have reached this area in 1348-49 and is thought to have killed between a third and half of the population by the time the disease had run its course in 1379. The prohibition for tenants not to leave the land broke down in the face of the Black Death, with people fleeing to try and escape the pestilence.

When the plague was over, the survivors had much more bargaining power, which eventually led to the break up of the feudal system. Labour service had to be paid for by the lord in wages to his former tenants and, as there was a surplus of land, rents went down. This may have been one of the reasons for the de Barri family selling up.

it was the home of a merchant from Tenby area. He also describes a house opposite the Palace which he calls the Place of Arms. Both the Palace and the Place of Arms are

# THE CHURCH BEFORE THE REFORMATION

When the Normans arrived in Manorbier, the Church would have been a Celtic church with a style of worship and procedures quite strange to them. The first Norman Bishop of St. Davids, Bernard, was appointed in 1115. He laid down the Diocesan structure that still exists. He created the two Parishes of Manorbier and Penally. Manorbier was probably dedicated to a Celtic Saint, perhaps St. Teilo. The dedication was changed to St. James the Great, and Norman or English priests would have been introduced to preach in the Norman way. Gerald de Barri, who was a reformer of the Celtic Church, had problems persuading the priests to pay the newly devised tithe of a tenth of the produce of the Parish. Another difficulty was that, far from being celibate, the Celtic priests kept mistresses and some were known to have 'willed' their benefices to their children. Gerald fought against this, and became Archdeacon of Brecon by forcing out the incumbent who was living with his 'concubine'.

Manorbier Church had an early connection with Monkton Priory, a Benedictine house founded by Arnulf de Montgomery, ten years after the Norman invasion of Pembroke-shire. The Priory was a daughter house of Seez Abbey in Normandy. The first recorded Rector of Manorbier was Master Richard in 1251 who was the Prior of Monkton. John de Barri granted the Church, with the Advowson and Glebe lands, to Monkton Priory in 1301. This was a valuable gift, as, besides the income from the rent, the Advowson, which gives the right to appoint the Rector, was valuable in itself. There are the remains of buildings south of the Church, which may have been a Grange or a Chantry. Church Cottage (now Priests Nose Cottage) has a pointed barrel vault over the interior, which suggests that it may be a medieval building.

After King John lost Normandy to the French in 1203, incomes from priories were still going to France. As England was frequently at war with France, these 'Alien' priories were given to other Abbeys, and Monkton Priory, with Manorbier Church and others, came under the rule of St. Alban's. Eventually, by an Act of 1414, they were taken into the King's hands. There Manorbier Church stayed until the reign of Henry VII.

# ABSENT LANDLORDS

Alice Perrers, who was lady-in-waiting to Queen Philippa, wife of Edward III, became the King's mistress after Queen Philippa died of the plague in 1369. Edward was almost sixty and he became infatuated with Alice who was about twenty-one. He gave her the jewels and robes of the dead Queen and she was said to have paraded through London wearing them. She also became involved in the politics of the time, and joined the judges on the bench when they were dealing with cases that involved her. This was disapproved of and she was banished from Court in 1376. She returned a year later following a plea from the dying King. She was said to have stolen the rings from his hand after death, and took anything else that was portable. She was banished again but returned later to the Court of Richard II, a wealthy woman. Alice Perrers purchased the Barony of Manorbier from the de Barri's sometime before 1392.

The Manorbier estate was just one of many properties owned by Alice Perrers who, after profiting from being the mistress of Edward III, became a very shrewd business-woman, and accumulated many estates. It is very unlikely that she lived at Manorbier, and may not even have visited, as the Estate would have been managed by an agent. Confusion arose about the ownership of the Estate on her death. King Henry IV ruled that John de Holand, the Duke of Exeter, should inherit Manorbier. Exeter was later beheaded for treason and his widow Elizabeth married Sir John Cornwall. In one of the few known preparations of Manorbier Castle for warfare, in September 1403, Sir John Cornwall was ordered by the King to defend Manorbier in the face of the Glyndŵr uprising. Manorbier was not attacked as Glyndŵr turned away.

By 1484, the Estate had again become Crown property and Richard III granted Manorbier to Richard Williams. He had been ordered to guard Milford Haven against any possible invasion by Henry Tudor and on the death of Richard III at Bosworth he disappears from history. Henry Tudor, now Henry VII, gave the estate to his mother, Lady Margaret Beaufort in 1487 (*Plate 5*).

Margaret suffered a life of considerable vicissitude. After a childhood betrothal that had been dissolved, she, a great heiress, was married at twelve years old to the twenty-six-year-old Edmund Tudor in 1455. It was normal practice to wait until the wife was fourteen before consummating the marriage, but Edmund had a very good reason to make her pregnant straight away, as, once a living child was born, he was then legally entitled to enjoy his wife's estates until his death. Not that it did him much good as he died before his son, Henry, was born. Margaret never had another child and her main ambition was for her son to become King. She married a second time to Lord Stafford in 1457. This marriage seems to have been happy until his death in 1471.

Her third and final marriage was to Thomas Lord Stanley in 1472. Margaret plotted against Richard III, and in 1483, as punishment, most of her estates were assigned to her husband for his life, which meant they would revert to the King on Stanley's death. Crucially, she persuaded her husband to support her son Henry Tudor against the King. At the battle of Bosworth in 1485, Thomas Stanley and his brother changed sides during the battle, ending the life and reign of Richard III.

After Henry's victory, Margaret won back the estates that she had lost during the reign of Richard III. It is doubtful that Margaret was entitled to the Manorbier estate but Parliament confirmed to her the manorial rights.

Margaret founded Christ's College, Cambridge, in 1505. She decided to grant the College the lands and Advowson of St. James Church, Manorbier, in 1508. This was worth £93, but to grant it to the College she had to compensate the Rector of Manorbier with an annuity of £30. The College remained responsible for the upkeep of the Church's chancel until 1920. Generously, Christ's College donated funds towards the repair of the Chancel in 1985.

After Margaret's death in 1509, the Manor reverted to the Crown, and was eventually granted by Henry VIII to his bastard son, Henry Fitzroy, in 1525, when he was six years old. This boy, Henry's only living son at the time, was also given a Dukedom and other honours, and it is thought that Henry VIII may have been planning to make him his heir. After his divorce from Catherine of Aragon to marry Anne Boleyn in 1533, any plans the King had for his son were abandoned. Henry Fitzroy died in 1536 aged seventeen. The Manor of Manorbier and Penally had been leased out before Fitzroy died, and was eventually leased to Hugh Jones for twenty years. He had been a Page of the King's chamber. The annual rent was £93-6s-8d (about £29,000 now). This must have been too much for Hugh Jones, who died in the Fleet prison sometime before 1550, owing the king £213.

The lease was assigned in 1590 to Sir Gelly Meyrick, a Pembrokeshire man and right-hand man to Robert Devereux, Earl of Essex. After the failure of the Essex conspiracy against Elizabeth I, the Earl was beheaded and Sir Gelly Meyrick was hung, drawn and quartered. His brother, Sir Francis, had arrived in London after the failure of the rebellion. He had to explain his arrival in London at that time and used the excuse that he was meeting his brother to discuss problems with the Manorbier estate. This may have been the case for there is a letter that was written by

Sir Francis to his brother a few years earlier referring to problems about 'the Manerbyre men'.

The Estate was leased on 14th December 1601 to Thomas Bowen of Trefloyne, who had been Steward of the Manorbier Estate, which included Penally at the time. The lease was for thirty-one years, backdated to 26th March 1601. This seems to have been a straightforward change of lessee, but in a court case brought by his son Charles Bowen against Nicholas Gwyther in 1609, it was stated that Sir Gelly's younger brother, Sir Francis, should have held the lease. Sir Francis was then in trouble over the Essex revolt and Thomas Bowen got the lease 'by some suttle means'. Charles Bowen was involved in several court cases, mainly against the Gwythers of East and West Moor. One case accused him of trying to de-populate the estate and convert most of it into pasture for sheep and cattle. Some-time before 1618 King James I sold the estate and Charles Bowen became the owner. He left the estate to his son Thomas when he died in 1640.

During Thomas Bowen's ownership of the Estate the Civil War broke out in 1642. Thomas Bowen was thought to have been a supporter of the Royalist cause but in a letter written in 1645 he complained that he had been plundered of all his wealth. After the fighting had stopped in 1646 a petition was sent to Parliament on his behalf by leading men of the County. This petition stated that the Royalists had invaded his property, driven him out, and fortified it for themselves and he was claiming compensation from the victorious Parliament who had destroyed Trefloyne.

Thomas' brother-in-law, Sampson Lort, of East Moor, was a younger brother of Roger Lort of Stackpole. These two brothers seem to have changed their allegiance during the Civil War to suit their own situations and probably Thomas Bowen followed them with his own changes in support.

One of the other major landowners, Will Marichurch of Norchard, was a Royalist and an officer helping to man Pill Fort on the Haven. When the Fort was captured by the Parliamentarians in 1644, he was imprisoned until the end of the First Civil War in 1645.

At Manorbier Castle, which was semi-ruined, the Royalists built earthworks to protect the gatehouse but there is no evidence that the Castle was attacked. After the battle of Colby Moor in August 1645, when Carew Castle surrendered to Parliamentary forces, it is thought that the surrender of Manorbier was included as well.

When the Second Civil War broke out in 1648, the leaders of the Parliamentarians in Pembroke Castle amazingly changed sides, and supported the King. Fighting started again, and Thomas Bowen and Sampson Lort joined the rebel Royalists, in Bowen's case perhaps because he had received no compensation for the damage to his property. Will Marichurch appears to have been consistent in his support of the King's party. All three major landowners of Manorbier lordship were now supporting the Royalists.

Thomas Bowen was captured after the battle of St. Fagans, which the Royalists lost. They then retreated back to Pembroke Castle to await events. Oliver Cromwell and his Army arrived before Pembroke Castle in May 1648 and the Royalists surrendered in July. Cromwell then ordered that the castles of Pembrokeshire be slighted. A committee was formed to carry out this task and somehow Sampson Lort became a member of the three man committee.

Although he supported the Royalist side, Will Marichurch does not appear to have been directly affected after the war ended and Norchard was never fortified or attacked. Samson Lort appears to have changed sides a few times, and finished up with the winners, being trusted by Cromwell to help carry out the demolition of the castles, and East Moor does not appear to have been fortified or attacked. Thomas Bowen may have stayed on the losing side. He seems to have lost large sums of money, and his house at Trefloyne had been destroyed.

Eventually, after his death in 1650, the Estate was then passed to his son, another Thomas. The Estate was sold in 1670 to Sir Erasmus Philipps of Picton Castle for £6,000 (now worth £500,000). Part of the agreement included Thomas's marriage to the eldest daughter of Sir Erasmus. The descendants of the Philipps family still own what remains of the original de Barri Estate.

# THE DEVELOPMENT OF THE FARMS

After the Black Death finished its ravages at the end of the fourteenth century, the villages and farms began to recover and the population started to increase again. With there no longer being a resident Lord of the Manor the absentee Lords wanted as much profit from their property as possible. This led them to let out their Demesne Lands, with the village lands also being rented from the Lord.

The separate estate of Norchard was the first independent farm within the Manor and was in existence before 1360. It seems to have been a rather special case as it had a payment of half a Knight's fee, which compares to the five Knight's fees that the de Barri family originally owed for the whole of the Manor. This became four and a half Knight's fees later, presumably because Norchard was paying the other half. Knight's fees had changed to become a yearly rent to the Lord, rather than a force of five fighting Knights. Norchard House has medieval barrel vaults in the core of the building, which points to the house's antiquity.

The first known owner of Norchard was Thomas Looney, also spelt Lynny and Lang. The Marichurch family became the owners in about 1440 and continued until about 1670 when the male line failed and Mary Marichurch married John Williams of Gumfreston in 1673. They had two daughters, who married two brothers, Mary to John Meyrick, and Alice to Francis Meyrick. In this way, both the Norchard and Gumfreston estates came into the ownership of the Meyrick family of Bush, descendants of Sir Francis Meyrick, brother of Sir Gelly. Five of the Marichurch family served as Mayors of Tenby in the early sixteenth century.

The first farm formed out of the Demesne Lands was 'the More parcel' sometime before 1550. As the name implies, the farm was on moorland which would have needed improvement by the tenant. At some stage it was split into separate farms, East and West Moor. In 1630 John Gwyther bought both East and West Moor farms from the Bowens. Later, Sampson Lort, brother of Henry Lort of Stackpole Court, settled at East Moor, and became High Sheriff of the County in 1650, just after the Civil War. He died in 1667 and his only son, Thomas, succeeded him at East Moor. He died without children and the farm was sold, and in 1786 was owned by Sir Hugh Owen.

An inventory of the possessions of Thomas Lort after his death in 1687 mentions the following rooms in East Moor: "hall, the little room within the hall, the little parlour, chamber over the outward kitchen, 'another little room', closet, little room over the entry, chamber over the kitchen, closet within the said chamber, buttery, kitchen, outer kitchen, larder, dairy and outhouses."

Three Surveys of the Manorbier Estate were taken between 1601 and 1618. These were to resolve the rights of the various type of tenant, but they give a good picture of the farms at that time. The Surveys list the names of the tenants, acreages farmed, types of tenancies and various other information. By the time of the Surveys in the early 1600's, there were hardly any Demesne Lands remaining, apart from the land at the Castle, a park of about seventy acres and a strip of land called the Lords Mead at Manorbier Newton.

In 1617 'or thereabouts' John Bishop of Manorbier Newton made his last will and testament. He gave his son Henry ten pounds (about £1,000 today) and his niece Elizabeth one ewe and a lamb. The rest of his goods and chattels he bequeathed equally to his wife Jennett and to a David Bishop whose relationship to John Bishop is unknown. The will was not written down, signed and witnessed at the time, but was reported as the spoken intentions of the dying man by witnesses after the event. Normally this was done a few months after the death, but in this case seven years went by before the inventory was drawn up and another year before probate was declared. The executors were his wife and David Bishop. The will was witnessed by "Robt Rudd parson of St fflorence and Robt Smith of the same towne."

The inventory of John Bishop's property gives the value of his corn in the haggard, crops in the field, his livestock, his farm equipment, and the furniture in his house.

His farm was of about thirty acres. He grew wheat and peas and kept cattle, sheep, pigs and horses, together with a few geese and hens. He owned a cart, a plough and two harrows with a shovel and pitchfork.

The furniture in his house was very sparse with only a settle, table and two forms, three chests and an old cupboard, with no bed, but some bedding. He had three brass pans, six pewter dishes and three candlesticks. There was also an iron grate, a spit, some brewing barrels and a churn.

The annual rent for his land was £1-3s-2d (£110 present value). The value of his haggard of corn and his crops was £6-13s-4d, his livestock £12-8s-8d and his farm equipment was £3-18s. The furniture and household goods were valued at £5-15s-1d. It is very difficult to compare this in any way with our present living conditions. Even people who are now considered to be in extreme poverty have a vast amount more than this reasonably successful farmer. Perhaps the only valid comparison is with the then Vicar, William Prichard, whose income was £8 per year and who was regarded as comfortably off.

By 1601, farms had been created within the Demesne which are still in existence today. They are Calvesland, Skrink Hill (Skrinkle), Hill and Norton which all lay outside the village fields. In the sale agreement of 1670 to Sir Erasmus Philipps, the farms at Skrinkhill and Hill are included, as is a farm at Ludsope (Lydstep), with the Mill, the Castle and Park, together with several dwelling places in the Manor of Manorbier.

The Manorial Court records for the Manor of Manorbier from 1686 to 1698 still survive. They refer to the tenants in Manorbier only, for Penally, although in the same Manor, had its separate Courts. The freeholders of Manorbier and Penally had their own Court at Longstone, which was the Standing Stone on the Norchard land. The Manorial Courts were held twice a year, in the spring and autumn, and in the autumn Court, three Reeves were chosen for Manorbier, Jameston and Manorbier Newton to collect the tenant's rents. The Court records show that a lot of the land was changing hands at this time, with people buying and selling tenancies in the village fields of Jameston and Manorbier Newton. This is totally different from the situation shown during the Surveys of 1601 to 1618. More land seems to have become available, and the fields of both Jameston and Manorbier Newton increase in size, with tenants combining strips to make more manageable fields.

The early eighteenth century Trefloyne Rentals record Slade Farm, Manorbier Croft, Wall Park, Park and New

Park. All of these farms were in the Lord's Demesne but there were several other properties in the villages not mentioned by name. In 1805, Richard Fenton, during his tour of Pembrokeshire, said that the village of Manorbier consisted of a few inhabited cottages with a great number in ruins (*Plate 9*).

By the middle of the eighteenth century, many farms existed on the village fields, these being shown on maps of the Picton Estate, and named in the Land Tax records: Mud Moor, Middle Hill, Robin Cross, Tarr, Bier, Green Grove, New House, Rock, Sunny Hill, Beaver Hill, Baldwin's Moor, Holly Lake and Soger. The Tax Returns of 1831 record more names: Newton Cottage, Cow Park, Pound Walls, Kiln Park, Red House, Summer Hill, Coopers Lake, Landways and Slough.

There were active land improvements being undertaken in Pembrokeshire during the early 19th century. Lord Milford, previously Sir Richard Philipps, was encouraging his tenants to add lime to the land to improve it by putting in requirements for limeing in any new tenancies. This explains the large number of lime-kilns spread about the parish, with almost every farm having its own kiln, as the advantage of limeing was recognised. Mr. Thomas Lewis at Norchard was one of the active enthusiasts of new methods of farming, and arranged ploughing matches on his farm in the 1840's. He also won prizes for his Southdown sheep.

By the 1841 Census more farms are named including Swan Lake, Clay Park, Buttyland, West Slade, Redhouse, Newton Hill, East Mead, Spring Hill, Kiln House, Bogg, Halfway House and Furzey Back and a few more are named in the 1851 Census including Newton Lodge, Winter Hill and West Heath. Most of these places are still recognisable today. These farms were in the main small, with about 20 to 30 acres of land, with some as little as 5 acres. This was at a time when Norchard Farm had 500 acres.

The coming of the railway to Manorbier in 1863 changed farming within the Parish because now livestock and produce could be moved by rail and artificial fertilisers could be brought into the county. There was a steady increase in the amount of machinery being used, beginning in the 1870's as a response to the scarcity and high cost of farm labour.

By 1871 a lot of the small farms had disappeared and been amalgamated into the larger ones, one example being Swan Lake, the ruins of which can still be seen when walking down to the bay. The number of farms continued to reduce, and by 1923, there were thirty farms with Windhill and Newton Cottage no longer recorded.

The process of small farms combining to make larger ones has continued to this day and we now have only about twenty working farms within the Parish. Most of the old farmhouses still stand but they are private homes, not farms.

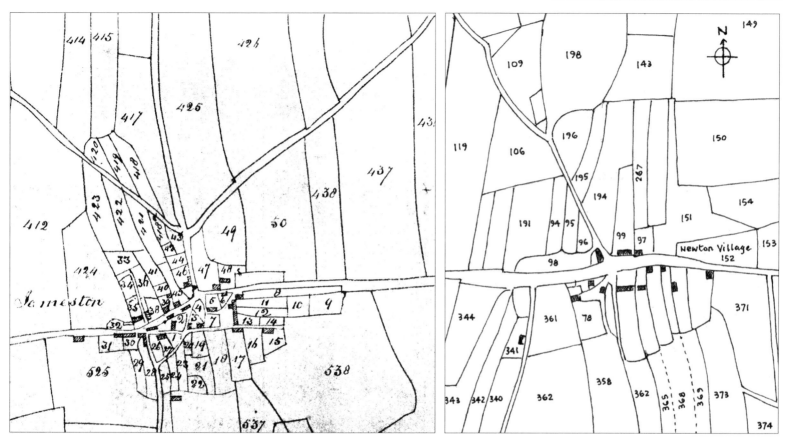

Tithes were primitive income tax to support the Church and originally a tenth of the annual value of the crops and animals. This system had become very confused by the beginning of the nineteenth century, so the amounts to be paid by each landowner were decided by Commissioners, appointed by the Government, based on the land owned. For this, maps were needed, and the earliest maps for Jameston and Newton are these, which were drawn in 1840.

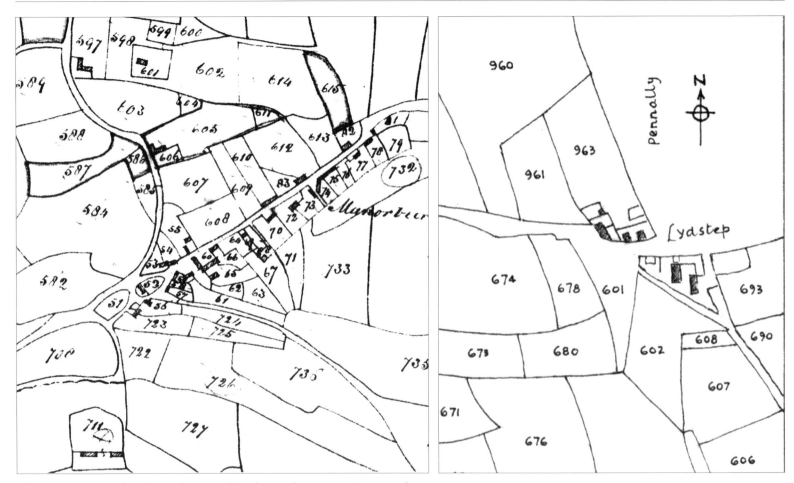

The Tithe maps for Manorbier and Lydstep drawn in 1840 are shown.

# THE DEVELOPMENT OF THE VILLAGES

The villages must have developed with the farms, although the information is very scarce until the detailed Censuses begin in 1841. The first evidence found for the sizes of the villages is in a Rental of 1485. This shows Manorbier with twenty-six holdings, Jameston with twenty-two, and Newton with sixteen. However, by the early seventeenth century, the villages may have shrunk slightly in size because, according to Professor R. F. Walker's study of the early seventeenth century surveys, Manorbier village had 22 dwellings, Jameston 18 and Manorbier Newton 14, this being a total of 54, with 7 outlying farms. He has also interpreted the descriptions in the surveys to conclude that Manorbier village had 8 substantial farms, 9 houses and 5 cottages, Jameston 7 farms, 10 houses and 1 cottage and Manorbier Newton 6 farms, 7 houses and 1 cottage. None of these village farms are recognisable in Manorbier, probably because of the nineteenth century changes, but three farms at Jameston and two at Manorbier Newton can still be recognised.

The surnames of the tenants show that English names predominate with Adams, Allen, Cole, Cook, Hilling, Hitching, Philps (now Phillips), Proute, Rogers, Rowe and Scourfield still common in the area. Some Welsh ones like Gwyther, Thomas and Williams had come into the parish.

The number of dwellings in the parish was 92 according to the Hearth Tax of 1670, which included the outlying farms. Interestingly, these not only showed the people liable to pay the Tax, but also Paupers who do not pay and they made up about a third of the population. The number of dwellings in the Parish had increased to ninety-seven in the Census of 1801.

The 1841 Census is the first exact information of the number of dwellings and population in the villages. Manorbier had 26 dwellings with a population of 103, Jameston had 37 dwellings and a population of 149, Manorbier Newton had 13 dwellings with a population of 68, and Lydstep had 9 dwellings with a population of 50, the first time that a village at Lydstep is recorded. The total number of dwellings in the Parish was 145, so there were now 60 farms and dwellings outside the villages.

Neither Manorbier nor Manorbier Newton had increased in size since 1485. By 1841 Jameston had almost doubled and was thriving. The village fields for Jameston were now about twice the area of those for Manorbier, with more land being brought under cultivation in the 17th century. The village had five shoemakers, a shopkeeper, a fishmonger, a cooper, a schoolmaster and a publican. There was also a school and a Primitive Methodist Chapel. Jameston Green or Fair was held every year, and a lot of the houses became unlicensed inns for the time of the Green. The village continued to thrive and thirty years later, although there was only one shoemaker, there were also two tailors, a dressmaker, two grocers, a laundress, a blacksmith and three innkeepers. Jameston people supported three inns, the Plough Inn, the Royal William, and the New Inn, which may have become the Railway and is now the Swan Lake Inn.

The railway had arrived in Jameston and there was a Halt at Beavers Hill crossing with a gatekeeper.

There was a shipwright living in the village who worked in the Royal Dockyard in Pembroke Dock. The Dockyard workers had to walk to work from Jameston. The Shipyard doctor covered his area on horseback and sometimes when he arrived at a cottage the 'ill' man would rush into the house and get into bed fully dressed. The doctor was concerned about the distance walked and the work needed to be done but one wife said: "Don't worry doctor, he gets plenty of rest at work." This story is backed up when one of the foremen at the Dockyard discovered a hidden resting place for the workers.

Thirty years later, in 1901, the tailor, shoemaker and blacksmith had disappeared. There were three dressmakers and four laundresses. A similar pattern appears in Manorbier Newton as in 1841 there were three cordwainers, a mantle maker, and a druggist. There was an Inn on the Ridgeway called Jenny Kibble's Pub. A cordwainer was a shoemaker and a mantle was a type of wrap or cloak. By 1871, there was a butcher, two dressmakers, and a railway crossing keeper. In 1901, there were no local tradespeople in business.

Manorbier village also had its skilled craftsmen and in 1841 there were two shoemakers, two tailors, two black-smiths, and a millwright. There were two inns namely the Castle and the Lion. Ten years later there were three inns, the Old Castle, the Lion and the Castle. In 1871, Manorbier had three shoemakers and a seamstress, together with a coachman, two nurses, a gardener, a ladies maid and two cooks. The Old Castle Inn had gone, the Lion was now a hotel, with only the Castle Inn remaining. In 1901 the census records more house staff in the village and there are two dressmakers, but only one bootmaker. Manorbier now had a schoolmaster, for the school which was opened in 1873.

Lydstep developed as a quarrying village with the quarry at Lydstep at its peak employing about 25 permanent workers. Lydstep House was built around 1810 for the Adams family of Holyland, near Pembroke, and they employed several staff. In 1841, there were carpenters, blacksmiths and servants, who were employed either at the quarry or at Lydstep House. An attempt was made in about 1870 to work a vein of fine potter's sand in Skrinkle Bay but a storm demolished the staging and the work was abandoned. With the enlargement of Lydstep House in 1894 by Lord St. Davids there is an increase in the number of service staff in the 1901 Census.

Iron ore was being worked in Jameston and Lydstep in the 1870's and used in the Saundersfoot Furnaces for several years. It was not of a very high quality and was mainly superseded by imported ore, and the 'Pembrokeshire Mining Syndicate, Manorbier' was closed in 1908.

Manorbier began to be developed in about 1870, with the building of large houses and villas for the gentry to spend their summers by the seaside. Most of the new buildings were built on the site of old cottages. A 'Tourist' in 1872 said that Manorbier may have been a larger village previously "judging from the number of fragments of old edifices strewn far around." He goes on to say that: "Until the last two or three years, tourist accommodation here was of a very limited and inferior description; recently, however, a few excellent houses have been erected in a delightful situation facing the bay."

# MURDER, SMUGGLING AND WRECKING

The parish of Manorbier has not always been the peaceful place that it is now. About two hundred years ago it was one of the major criminal centres in the country. Even earlier, in 1721, a crime occurred that changed the law of the land.

Thomas Athoe, a yeoman of Manorbier, was elected mayor of Tenby in 1721. During the November fair of that year, Thomas and his son quarrelled with his nephew, George Marchant, over the sale of some cattle. After the argument, the Athoes, father and son, lay in wait for George Marchant, who had his brother Thomas with him, and

George was murdered by the Athoes at Holloway bridge in Penally. Their defence was that the Marchants had stolen their land, cheated them out of cattle, and George had married the sweetheart of the young Athoe. The Athoes were taken to Hereford for trial as there was no chance of obtaining a conviction in Pembrokeshire with the whole of the County having taken their side, probably believing that George Marchant had deserved what he got. According to Edward Laws: "The very complicated arrangements to bring these ruffians to justice constitutes the chief interest in a very commonplace murder." It was not certain that criminals could be tried in a different county from that in which the offence had occurred so their case was brought before the Court of the King's Bench in Westminster Hall. The difficulty was resolved by a Special Act of Parliament which said: "that all murders and robberies committed in, on, or about the Borders of Wales should be triable in any county in England where the criminals were taken." This resolved the legal difficulty and the Athoes were tried, convicted, and later hanged on the boundary of London. They were the last criminals to be executed at that spot.

The Athoe and Marchant families were living in Manorbier Newton until the 1870's so the murder seems to have been forgotten by later generations.

During the Napoleonic Wars, in the late 18th to early 19th centuries, Manorbier was a centre for smuggling. The normal trading between Britain and France ceased due to the war and private enterprise took over. In 1801 the hero of the unsuccessful French Invasion six years earlier, Lord Cawdor, was knocked down in a struggle with smugglers at Freshwater East. The only smuggler caught was rescued by a mob who also took back some of the casks which had been impounded. The Revenue men struggled to halt the trade and, in April 1804, the tide-surveyor of Tenby and his boat crew seized 47 Ankers (8 gallon barrels) of contraband brandy.

The Rev. Sir Thomas Gery Cullum, Bart. visiting in July 1811 recorded how "of late years, the castle at Manorbier has been appropriated to smuggling on a most daring scale. The person concerned, having hired the castle of the farmer and having built a house contiguous, used to fill the subterranean chambers and towers with spirits. A number of casks were soon discovered floating in the reservoir. At last, after several seizures, this illicit trade was put a stop to by Lord Cawdor, who was nearly killed in the attempt." This possibility of someone hiring the Castle or a farm to carry out smuggling is reinforced by a story told to early tourists, Mr. and Mrs. S. C. Hall, who visited Manorbier Castle in 1860. They were told by an old man that "a stout-hearted smuggling gentleman took Manorbeer Park farm, an' purtended that he brought over five Cornishmen to teach our lads mining, an' our women to milk cows. It was sometimes carrying kegs over the rocks an' stones at Lydstep, an' hiding 'am in our caves there, or else taking a run with 'am up the green slopes to the men in waiting if the coast was clear. Many a boat have I seed upset in the surf of Manorbeer Bay, and then scramble – who scramble could! We had cellars all about the cliffs, two on Hill Farm, some under the old parsonage walls, by Manorbeer Church; an' bless you, the castle itself is like a mole-hill – the earth under it is full of our runs. Eh! If you had but seen the smuggling cutter, *Jane*, sailed by Captain Furze, and pursued by a King's ship, with the shot flying over us like hail in thunder, an' we bobbing like geese under an archway to 'scape it. 'Get down, my lads,' says Captain Furze, says he, 'get below; I'll balk him yet – the timber isn't spliced that'll run down Jack Furze – down my lads, at once!' An' as a spoke, a threw hisself flat on the deck, and so a steered lying on his back. He dodged from day till dark – when we came on deck, and making a suddan turn in his coorse, he 'scaped. Ah! Captain Jack was something, he was!" Allowing for some exaggeration by the old man to make his tale more impressive for his listeners, his story shows that people of the Parish knew about and were involved in this illicit trade.

The last authenticated record of smuggling in Pembrokeshire was in the summer of 1825 at Swanlake Bay. A Mr. Jenkins of Pembroke, who had a reputation for the 'unofficial' importing of goods, asked the farmer and his wife, who lived above the Bay, if he could store some cargo in their cellars. They agreed, but knowing of the large rewards offered for the capture of smugglers, decided to tell the Excise men. After the cargo was landed on Thursday night, his wife set out for Tenby on Saturday, but met a housewife in Manorbier who she told of her mission. The housewife was an old employee of Mr. Jenkins so she rushed to Pembroke and warned him. He gathered his men together, picking up others on the way, and removed the barrels to other safe houses. When the Excise men came on the Monday morning there was nothing to be found. After that the couple were not very popular in the neighbourhood, and were said to have left the farm soon afterwards.

The *Tenby and County News* of summer 1908 reported another story of smuggling in Manorbier which was published in the *Wide World* magazine. In it the writer, Mr. E. S. Gould, says that he found himself in Manorbier in early 1860 and being struck with the place managed to get a lease on the Castle which had been unoccupied since the death of its last owner, a London specialist, more than twenty years before (about 1840). He writes that: "It appeared that between forty and fifty years before the date of my purchase of the lease, a band of Cornishmen had suddenly appeared from across the Bristol Channel and having leased the Castle, started an elaborate and profitable system of smuggling, using the castle as a cache; whilst as a blind a cornmill and barns were built outside the walls and intermittent traffic for this commodity also carried on for years. The end of these wily little schemes seems to have come swiftly and dramatically, the cause being the appearance in the district of a more than usually strenuous member of the Excise. This enterprising young man apparently entered the Castle to search and was found a week later with broken skull at the foot of a shaft in one of the curtain towers. The sole member of the band in occupation was a lad of fifteen or so called Tregarthen who was found in the mill outside the walls. The boy was tried for murder forthwith but easily established an alibi having just returned from business in Bristol to find that his father, whom he had left alone in the place, had disappeared. The village folk were apparently good to the silent and rather morose boy for he found employment and he eventually became the host of the Castle Inn. The elder Tregarthen has never been heard of since."

Mr. Gould continues: "Billy Johns, the aged custodian of the Castle, had been so local rumour said, constantly startled by sights and sounds within the walls of which he could give no explanation. After visiting the Castle at night I saw a figure moving about the ruins and on giving chase discovered the water gate leading down to the sea unlocked and open. I summoned a friend from London, one Nolan, to help probe the mystery and three days later he arrived. The mystery was solved with unexpected suddenness. Sitting upon the battlement wall in the darkening gloom we were startled by a strange sight. The well in the courtyard nearly forty feet deep had no parapet and was covered with a sliding wooden door. The cover was now pushed back a foot or two and on the stone flagged edge rested two claw-like hands, whilst above them peered forth the most inhuman face we have ever seen. The appearance was but momentary and the head disappeared. Resolved to unravel the mystery we decided to descend the well. I was lowered first by means of a windlass, and Nolan following. At the bottom we found an archway leading to a tunnel, up which we groped our way. Our feeble light was sufficient to show us both that we now stood in a cave some twelve foot long by about the same in breadth, with the rock floor well above water level. The cave was evidently a cellar cut by hand from the solid rock and there could be no doubt that it had been the smugglers cache. Here and there lay huddled heaps of barrels and cases rotten with damp, and among them a few miners tools, but there were no other vestiges of human habitation. From this point I have a very sketchy recollection of subsequent events. I can recollect lifting the lantern to trim the wick, which had become clogged, and of half turning to speak to Nolan when without warning and quite silently, a black shape detached itself from the shadows and sprang at me, striking me heavily on the forehead with some blunt instrument. I remember the lantern went crashing against the wall and that I seemed to be falling an immeasurable distance, and then everything became a blank. Recovering consciousness some time later I learned that the man who had struck me had himself been killed. A living skeleton, bound in yellow buckram and bald as a coot, he had been dragged down to the floor of the cave and killed by the mere weight of the man whom he had assaulted falling on him. The mystery was, of course, easily solved. John Tregarthen, who had never been seen since the murder of the Excise officer, had lived for twenty years in the smugglers old store house, his whereabouts known only to his son the innkeeper, who had kept his father supplied with food. After these strange doings in the Castle, John Tregarthen the younger left the village never to be seen again."

Some of the above stories are authenticated and some are not, but even to this day the story of the cavern at the bottom of the well is regularly told. There seems to be nothing in the fairly rare early documentation to prove that Cornishmen rented the Castle, Park Farm, or any other property, but who knows?

There are rumours of wreckers in the coastal villages but the only evidence is a charge against several people, including a yeoman from Manorbier, of stealing from the sloop, *Two Partners*, which was wrecked in Lydstep Bay in 1762. Tales are told of lights that were tied on to the back of cattle and when these moved the lanterns would flash and the sailors on the ships were confused and thought that they were entering Milford Haven, by the time they realised their mistake it was too late and they ran into the rocks. They were apparently gangs of men waiting to take away any cargo. What happened to the sailors on the ships, the tales never say!

# RELIGION, CHURCH AND CHAPELS

Despite the lawlessness of some parts of the Parish, religion was a part of community life. Although the Church of England was established by Henry VIII in 1532, as late as 1620 John Gwyther of East Moor Farm was said to have harboured a Catholic priest. The Parish Church of St. James was where most people worshipped. A long-standing vicar was William Prichard whose tenure lasted from 1631 to 1675. He remained as vicar throughout the Civil War, the Protectorate and the Restoration of Charles II without upsetting anyone. This was more than his contemporary at St. Florence, Robert Rudde, managed, as he died after being imprisoned by the Parliamentarians.

In the Church, there is the Coat of Arms of William III, who as William of Orange, took the throne from James II in the 'Glorious Revolution' of 1688. This is the only example of this King's Coat of Arms in the County. The panel is made of planks of wood fastened together, with the Royal Arms painted on. Dated 1701, it shows the names of the two Churchwardens of that year, Edward Thomas and George Herbert, with the inscription, God bless King William, at the bottom. The name of Edward Thomas is also inscribed on the oldest Church bell dated 1698, when he was the only Churchwarden. A John Herbert is recorded as the Reeve of Jameston in 1697 in the surviving Court

Rolls for the Parish, so George Herbert is most likely a relative of his, possibly his son (*Plate 8*).

This display of support for William III was inspired by the death of James II in 1701. After his death, Louis XIV of France, who had sheltered James after his defeat by William at the Battle of the Boyne, recognised James' son as the rightful King of England. The whole country, outraged at the interference of the French King, strongly supported William, who, after the death of his wife Mary had not been very popular. The Coat of Arms in Manorbier demonstrates the Parishes' support for the Protestant King.

There was a vicarage near the Church, the remains of which can still be seen to the south of the path at the top of the new graveyard. In a letter from the Rural Dean to the Bishop of St. Davids in 1794, he states that the vicarage wants thorough repairs. He also says that of the 22 parishes in the Diocese, only 6 priests are resident. In 1841 Richard Leach, vicar of St. James for fifty years, was lodging at East Moor, as the vicarage was no longer habitable.

In about 1840 Manorbier Church gained a West Gallery for the choir and musicians. It did not meet with approval and was removed in 1849, replaced by pews and the West Window was installed. There was accommodation for 240 parishioners. Before these seats were installed those without their own pews had to stand at the back. When Christ College Cambridge, which owned the Advowson, made an inspection only five years later, in 1856, they discovered that the Church was in a very bad state with the pews rotten and the gutters letting in water. The then vicar, Henry Hughes, appeared to be more concerned about having a new vicarage built, together with a cottage for the school teacher. According to a 'Tourist' at that time ivy could be seen hanging from the roof entering every window and crevice.

At the College's next inspection in June 1858, just after a Mr. Crockford has been appointed as the new vicar, they pronounced that the Church was almost unfit for public worship. Astonishing if you consider that seven years earlier Henry Hughes claimed to have 240 worshippers in the Church. The Vicarage near to the Church had not been lived in for about sixty years and a new vicarage was proposed to be sited within the village. Mr. Crockford and his family were living in Tudor Lodge and were settled there so he asked that the construction of the vicarage be delayed. The Church was in such a bad condition that there was serious discussion about building a new Church in the village near to the new vicarage site. The attendance at St. James was very small, due to the difficulty for elderly people walking up the steep hill, and also because of the damp and cold interior.

In 1864 Henry Lamb became vicar and it was during his incumbency that the Church was restored and the vicarage (now known as the Old Vicarage) built. Work on the Church commenced in 1867 and was completed in a year at a total cost of around £1,400. The architect was F. Wehnert of Milford Haven and London. The Church benefited from a new chancel roof, east window and seats. Most of the old Elizabethan rood loft did not survive, and a new screen was installed across the Chancel. The remaining part of the rood loft, which is the oldest remaining woodwork in the County, was fitted above the east end of the north aisle. St. James Church was re-opened in August 1868 by the Bishop of St. Davids, Connop Thirlwall. Afterwards, luncheon was served in the Castle's chapel for the Bishop, clergy and parishioners. During the lunch, the Bishop remarked that he thought that Manorbier Church was one of the most interesting churches in Pembrokeshire.

The graveyard to the north of the church was extended down to the road in 1870, after a gift of the land by the Meyricks of Bush, and the old quarry of the Picton Estate provided the stone to build the wall.

The Church Sunday School was thriving in 1909, when well over one hundred children, teachers and parents were taken to Saundersfoot on their annual outing. Sports and games were arranged and a tea was given to them, all due to the generosity of Mr. and Mrs. Parcell.

The Choir outing of 1910 was also unlikely to be soon forgotten. They travelled on a Motor Bus from Manorbier at 8.30 a.m. and reached Roch Castle at 1.30 p.m. where they were treated to a tour of the castle and then sat down to "a right royal spread" given by the Hon. Roland Philipps,

the younger son of Lord St. Davids. They then travelled north "where the sight of a Motor Bus caused as much excitement as the landing of an Aeroplane." They went on and visited St. Davids Cathedral, were shown round and given tea, eventually arriving back in Manorbier at 4 a.m. They sympathised with their drivers as "twenty-four hours driving would tax the strength and temper of most men, but both seemed equal to all emergencies."

George Fox, the founder of the Quaker Movement, visited Tenby in 1657 and by the end of the seventeenth century there was a Quaker Community in Jameston. They were holding regular monthly meetings in 1714 but they were discontinued in 1777. Sadly, the Friends burial ground at Jameston has now been lost.

A Congregationalist Church began in Manorbier Newton in 1802 which eventually joined with Pembroke to found the Tabernacle there in 1812. The Congregationalists of Manorbier Newton leased land to build a Chapel, which was built in 1822. The lease, given by Mrs. Elizabeth Phillips, was for 99 years at 1 shilling per year. Rev. Benjamin Evans from St. Florence became Pastor and he was also responsible for building a Chapel in Tenby. When the Tenby Chapel was finished he had to give up Manorbier Newton and moved to Tenby. The next minister was Rev. James Eddy. In 1851 he claimed an attendance of 120. Certainly, under his ministry, Manorbier Newton was at its most successful. When he left, due to a disagreement, most of the congregation separated and dispersed. When Rev. Jason Jenkins came to St. Florence Chapel, he also looked after the few remaining members of Manorbier Newton, and the membership increased again, and a Sunday School was formed. The numbers in the congregation reduced after the Second World War, although the Sunday School was still active in 1957, arranging a visit to Saundersfoot as seen below.

*Back row, left to right: Heather Cole; Hazel Cole; George Gooch; Brenda Cole; Jimmy Gooch; Brian Cole. Middle row: ??; Helen Minchin. Front row: Michael Cole; Sheila Minchin; Sandra Day; Florence Gooch; Anthony Cole.*

However, in 1965 the membership was too few to continue, and the Chapel was closed, sold for £100 and converted to a holiday home.

The Primitive Methodist Chapel at Jameston was built on land owned by John Shears opposite the Swan Lake Inn. By 1851, they claimed an attendance of 60 members with John Bittle as the Chapel Steward. This did not last and in 1865 the Pembroke circuit decided that the Chapel should be sold as: "We go to preach time after time and get no congregation. No members, no money." It was eventually sold to the Wesleyans sometime before 1878 and continued in use until 1918, then it, too, was closed, sold and converted into a house, Chapel House.

The last of the nonconformist chapels to be built within the Parish was the Penuel Baptist Church which is still in use. The local Baptists obtained the site in 1848. The lease was signed for ninety-nine years at a ground rent of only two shillings per year and William Freeman, a stonemason and member, built the church. The attendance in 1851, one year after the church opened, was claimed to be 130 in the afternoon and 200 in the evening. The Deacon was William Freeman, the stonemason, and the Manager was James Cook. The first minister in 1853 was Benjamin Evans who may have been the grandson of the Pastor at Manorbier Newton. Under the Rev. John Thomas, appointed in 1880, there was a thriving Sunday School with eighty children. While he was at Penuel, the church was renovated and the roof re-built and heightened so that another level could be built. Unfortunately, after he left in 1888, his successor, Rev. John Harrington, had to deal with the problem of the walls not being strong enough to hold the roof and buttresses were built on the side of the Chapel to support the walls. He is said to have paid for these out of his own pocket. His ministry continued until 1898 and he and his family continued to live at Tudor Lodge where he farmed 50 acres. He was succeeded by Rev. C. Penrose who stayed until 1905. His successor was Rev. E. Jenkins who had a qualification in advanced phrenology, which was supposedly the science of reading bumps on people's heads to judge their ability. His Deacons were Edwin Minifrie, Thomas Gwynne, George Johns and William Freeman.

The Baptists continued with the membership varying between 30 to 70. Mrs. Glynne Parry, whose great, great grandmother was the sister of Rev. Benjamin Evans, remembers attending the church as a young girl when the organist was Miss Annie Harrington, daughter of a previous pastor, who would encourage the congregation's singing with cries of "Come on, keep up there, keep up, no slacking." The membership increased during the Second World War with the Artillery Range and evacuees increasing the numbers. At the end of the War the Pastor resigned, and there was a crisis at the Church as many evacuees left the village to go home and service men and women from the Range were demobbed. In 1953, Archibald Penrose, the son of the Pastor in the late 19th century, became the new Pastor, and with the help of the Secretary, Mr. Atkinson, increased the membership again.

*Early photograph of Penuel Baptist Church*

A hall was built alongside the Church in the early 1960's and used for social occasions. This hall has recently become a place of worship for the Emmanuel Gospel Church. Penuel Baptist Church celebrated their 150th anniversary in the year 2000.

A cottage in Jameston was given to representatives of St. James Church for use as a Mission Room in 1896. The cottage had originally been owned by John Tudor, who lived at what is now Tudor Lodge, and was given by his grand-children, who inherited it under the trust of his will. The property was to be used as a Parochial Mission and a Sunday School and was entrusted to the care of four trustees who were the Master of Christ's College, Cambridge, the Vicar of St. James Church and two church members, Robert Greenish and William Parcell, who were generous benefactors. The cottage was altered to make it more suitable for its new use and new windows, door, roof, bellcote and a small extension to make a chancel were added.

The Mission Hall was intended to encourage the residents of Jameston and Manorbier Newton to return to the Anglican Church, there being three Nonconformist Chapels in the Parish. It was well received for, with regular services and a Sunday School in Jameston, there was no longer the necessity for the long walk and steep climb to St. James Church. Over time the numbers attending the Mission Hall declined, the Sunday School was closed in the 1980's, and

*Jameston Mission Hall*

with a congregation of only three remaining, the decision was taken to close the Mission Hall in December 1998.

The formation of the Church in Wales was voted for just before the First World War, but the enactment was delayed until the end of the War. This change had been fought for by the nonconformists for many years for several reasons. One of the problems was the tithe system, in which a tenth of the produce of every farm was given to the Church. This was changed to a rental in 1836, with the tithe payments fixed for each farm. The incumbent of the parish had to collect the tithe rents, which job he often gave to his church warden. The nonconformists did not want to pay money to the church. A farmer in Jameston refused to pay his tithe rent, so the Picton agent, who was his landlord, came to the farm, removed two bullocks and tried to sell them locally. The only bid he received was "a pair of old boots", so they were taken to Haverfordwest where they were sold. After 1891, the responsibility for paying the tithe rental was given to the landlord, so the opposition to the payments died down.

The governing body for the parish was the Church Vestry, which nominated the Poor Law Guardians who looked after the poor, made sure the roads were kept in repair and various other responsibilities. However, the Vestry was chaired by the Vicar of the Church, and to be a member of the Vestry one had to be a member of the Established Church. This meant that nonconformists could not be involved in Parish government.

Another concern of the non-conformists was that the only schools available for their children to attend were Church schools, and this had been the case in Manorbier since 1873. Before that, there had been a private school in Jameston, and a Church school in Manorbier. For Manorbier Church, the disestablishment meant the end of the right to appoint the incumbent of the parish by Christ's College Cambridge, which had existed since it was given to the College by Margaret Beaufort in 1508. The last vicar appointed by the college was the Rev. Percy Rigby, who was Chaplain at the dockyard in Pembroke Dock before he was given the living of Manorbier.

# EDUCATION

In 1833 a private school was established in Jameston, which was the first school in the parish. Lessons were held in a room of a dwelling house, 14ft. square, but it is not known where the house was sited. In the Census of 1841, William Davies, 66, was described as a Schoolmaster. According to the Commission of Enquiry into the State of Education in Wales, published in 1847, he had worked as a labourer and as well as teaching, rented two fields and kept two cows. The school's income of eight pounds was financed from

School Pence, collected from the parents of the twenty children on the register. When the Commissioner's assistant, David Lewis, visited the school on 22nd December, he reported: "It was held in a room, part of a dwelling house, and lighted by one small glazed window about 15 in. square. The furniture consisted of three small tables, eight chairs and two low benches. There was a culm fire in the room, and the steam rising from it when I entered was almost intolerable. I examined some copy-books, and the writing, for children so young and with so few advantages, was very fair. Five children read the 23rd. chapter of Deuteronomy. One (a little girl) read pretty well; but all the boys very ill. The children were excessively ignorant, rude and ill- behaved. I could scarcely get a question answered. Knew who made the world. Did not know who Jesus Christ was. Had never heard of the Virgin Mary. Did not know how many Apostles there were. Had never heard of our Saviour coming on earth. The master here remarked that: 'It is something like remarkable that you reads and hears sermons, and don't recollect nothing that you sees and hears'."

St. James Church formed their school in 1841 in the building still to be seen just above the Church, now called Priests Nose Cottage. The first schoolmaster was a Dr. Lewis, who was paid £13 per annum. In 1846, the school's income was £25 a year, funded by subscriptions and donations. There were forty children on the register and there was a new schoolmaster. David Lewis visited Manorbier school on the same day as Jameston: "very substantially built, lighted by three glazed windows. The furniture consisted of desks round the room on the national system – one desk for the master, and one large one in the middle of the room, with benches, all in very good repair. The building was lofty, ceiled and well ventilated. There was a comfortable fire in the room. The master was an intelligent man. He had been a tailor, but from ill-health had been obliged to change his occupation. I heard the children read

the second chapter of St. Matthew's Gospel – five of the class (which was composed chiefly of girls) read very well and four others not at all ill. They answered my questions in Scripture history readily, and the answers in mental arithmetic by one boy in particular, were very good; three could repeat their Catechism pretty well, but did not seem to understand what they were repeating. Could not tell what two things were to be learnt from the Ten Commandments."

There was also a private school at Sunny Hill for about twenty years from 1841. This was not visited by the Commission. The school took boarders and was presumably intended for the children of more wealthy parents.

When the Government eventually decided that it would have to provide universal education, the Manorbier School we now know was built in 1873. The new school was built on land donated by Thomas Meyrick of Bush House: "for use as a school for the education of children of the labouring, manufacturing, and other poorer classes in the parish of Manorbier, and for no other purpose and that such school shall always be conducted according to the designs of the National Society for promoting the education of the poor in the principles of the Established Church." This definition naturally upset the nonconformists. After the school was built, the other two schools in the parish were closed.

The new school opened on Monday, 13th January 1873. The first master was James Quarterman and forty-eight names were registered. In 1973 for the school Centenary a

*The School in 1873*

small booklet was produced with extracts from the School Log:

1873 Manorbier National School.
Master: James Quarterman.

*13th Jan:* Today our school was opened with prayer and praise, the Rev. Phillips of St. Florence conducted the service, in the absence of the Rev. J. Lamb, vicar, who was disabled by an accident from attending. All the committee were present and also a number of parents notwithstanding the wet weather. Forty-eight names were registered. After the names were entered, I spoke a few words to the parents on regularity, punctuality, obedience and tale bearing.

*3rd April:* Very small school. About 24 absent to go to the "races" at Westmoor.

*21st May:* Detained Edw. Hughes for irreverent conduct at prayers, Wm. Matthews for indecency, W. Brooks for misbehaviour and three boys for jostling about uproariously when assembling to their lines.

*4th July:* A revolution! On coming into school at 1.15 I found the front door fastened and a stool placed against it, the lower door at which I entered was also partially barred. The delinquents, after a caution, were made to stand out in front of the desk until 3.30 to do their work and detained to write the word "contrivance" until 4.30.

*4th September:* A treat! Half Holiday! Capt. and Mrs. Versturme most generously opened their residence here by giving a treat to the school children. One hundred of them were entertained at Castle Mead. We took tea in front of the house and had many amusements in the meadow. On approaching the house two hymns were sung and on leaving also- with three hearty cheers for Capt. and Mrs. Versturme.

1874
*12th Nov:* Punished F. Llewellin with cane for beating R. Rixon and pushing pencil case up his nose.

1875
*March:* Mr. Quarterman resigned and Mr. Cornelius Wood became the teacher.

*15th June:* A few minutes before two o'clock Mr. Webbe the station master, came to the school and complained of an annoyance caused by a number of the children congregating at the railway station, obstructing himself and passengers and endangering lives. Every child late. Found that a meeting had been arranged at the station by the late teacher through the paid monitor. Detained seventy-nine children for being late at the station until five o'clock and the monitor about half an hour later.

## 1878
*16th October:* School treat kindly given by Mrs. Cobb of Manorbier Castle. The children met at the Castle Green at 3 o'clock and marched into the Castle to the Chapel. They were allowed to disperse and visit the most interesting parts. The ascent of the towers particularly pleased the children. After receiving buns from Mrs. Cobb they were taken to the sands and amused for nearly an hour returning to school for an excellent tea. After tea they sang a number of school songs and Mrs. Cobb presented prizes for sewing. This brought to an end a very happy day.

## 1879
*1st December:* School not opened, an outbreak of diphtheria in the parish. Dr. Saer recommended that the managers closed the school since last Friday four children had died: Elizabeth Thomas, Florence Thomas, Catherine Thomas and Mary Anne Allen.

*9th December:* Three other children dead: George Allen, Elizabeth Allen and George Thomas.

*19th December:* Two others have died: William Thomas, and William Nicholl.

## 1880
*12th January:* School reopened, parish apparently free from disease. Attendance very small.

## 1882
*3rd November:* Punished John Nicholls for making water in John Smith's bag.

## 1883
*1st October:* Punished J. Walters, J. Hughes and J. Phillips for plundering the vicar's orchard.

## 1886
*26th January:* Very heavy snow all night. Very deep this morning, no scholars present at 9 a.m. Five came between ten and eleven a.m. their feet dripping wet. Sent them home at once.

*2nd March:* Thomas Rogers, first standard, appeared in school this morning with a severe black eye and cut nose, the result of stone throwing against Joseph Warlow. I am sorry to say that these fights are common now. The master is not allowed to stop them or to punish the boys and girls who take part in them. Many have said that it is dangerous to pass the school children when they are quarrelling. When the master took charge of the school, he put down the stone throwing fights by severely punishing the boys who did so, but now "his hands are tied."

*20th July:* In consequences of the death of Mrs. Smith, the school mistress, it having been necessary to procure a mistress for the infants and sewing, it was agreed that Mary Jane Johns be engaged at a salary of £10 for the first year, £15 for the second year and £20 for the third, always providing that Her Majesty's Inspector is satisfied with her work.

1902
*26th June:* Feast, sports, fireworks held this day to celebrate the Coronation of Edward VII. These were held at Park.

1915
*10th November:* Vicar took first class in Scripture. A number of the boys and girls went down to Buttyland Farm at playtime this morning as a threshing machine was there. They were punished.

1916
*3rd June:* News heard of great Naval Battle (Jutland).

*Manorbier pupils, late 19th century*

*6th June:* News heard of Lord Kitchener's death. The children had a lesson on the naval battle and, although I had a very poor voice, I addressed all the children in the main room for forty minutes on Lord Kitchener's life and work. We have a short daily talk on the events of the war.

1919
*15th April:* Dead whale on sands at Manorbier Bay.

1920

*16th February:* Received circular from Pembs. Agric. Executive Committee on "Concerted rat destruction" which I read and explained to the children.

*2nd March:* During the week some of the boys have destroyed 90 rats, their names were sent up to Haverfordwest.

1922

*23rd January:* The whooping cough epidemic has developed rapidly. School closed until Monday, March 13th.

*13th March:* Reopen school with 55 children present out of 94.

1928

*17th July:* Owing to the sand carts being engaged on the hay, drinking water has only been obtainable through the courtesy of Buttylands Farm and the station master.

1932

Only twenty-three children present this afternoon, the remainder have stayed to watch an aeroplane which landed near Jameston during the dinner hour.

*16th Nov:* Mrs. Harries, the school cleaner, was discovered drowned in the rainwater tank at the rear of the premises during school this morning.

1941

*24th February:* Work started on the erection of an air raid shelter in the playground.

1949

*26th April:* The school reopened today after the Easter holiday and Mr. Ensor Morgan took charge as the newly appointed headmaster. The Rev. Garfield Davies was present at the opening. Number on Roll 43.

1956

The new classrooms were officially opened today in the presence of many parents, school managers and local Councillors and their wives, and Ald. B. G. Howells, Chairman of the Education Committee. The Rev. Garfield Davies led the gathering in prayer. During the ceremony the children sang two songs.

1959

*17th September:* Workmen started to install an electric supply in the school today.

1969

*1st July:* School holiday today to mark the Investiture of Prince Charles as Prince of Wales.

1970
We break up for the summer holiday today. This is my last entry. After 21 years and 3 months, I say good-bye and go into retirement. Ensor Morgan.

1973
*12th February:* Message of good wishes sent to the Queen on the occasion of the school's centenary.

Concerts were sometimes given in the school and a report in 1890 describes a concert which was held on behalf of the Church choir fund. The heavy rain on the night did not prevent a large crowd from attending. The evening was arranged by Mr. and Mrs. William Parcell and her brother, Mr. Arthur Greenish. All the items on the programme were well received. Songs were sung by Miss T. Parcell, Miss Wilkinson, Miss Smith and Mr. J. A. Roberts. Mr. Custances sang humorous songs and sang 'Plantation Songs' with a tambourine and castanet obligato. The entertainment also included a comic duet by Messrs. Roberts and Greenish and Master Percie Parcell recited 'Swanage Bay', with "charming simplicity and self-possession."

The school, now a Primary school, is still on the same site and it was from the outset controlled by the Church at Manorbier. Even after the changes in education over the years, the Church still has an involvement as it is a Voluntary Controlled School by the Church in Wales, and St. James Church supplies two members to the Governing Body.

# ROADS AND RAILWAYS

The original road serving the villages in the parish was The Ridgeway, which was the road used for centuries to get safely from Tenby to Pembroke. The roads from the Ridgeway went down to the villages and tracks went to the village fields. The parish was responsible for the repair of the roads to the Ridgeway and within the parish, and in the Court Rolls of the late 1600's, the parishioners of Manorbier Newton are digging clay for the highway in an attempt to repair it. In the Court Rolls, plots of land are sometimes described using roads as boundaries, these being the Newton to Pembroke road, the Jameston to Hodgeston road, the Manorbier to Lydstep road and so on, so there were then roads being used to get to the surrounding villages. The roads of Pembrokeshire were notoriously bad. Some turnpike roads were built but none in the Parish. These led to the Rebecca Riots, with rioters breaking down the turnpike gates. Troops were sent in to put down the riots and this alerted the government to the bad state of the roads, and a County Roads Board was set up in 1844. Improvements were made to connect roads to the railway stations on the new Tenby to Pembroke railway, and the newly arrived motor car required better roads. After the First World War, the road classification was decided by the volume of traffic. By then, motorists had decided that it was more convenient to go through the villages rather then using the Ridgeway, and it was not classified.

When the dock was opened in Pembroke Dock in 1814 better transportation was essential as it took around thirty hours by road from London. Various proposals for a railway were floated and eventually the Pembroke to Tenby Railway Company was formed in 1859. The railway line was constructed by Davies and Roberts who not only built the line but also provided the finance. The line opened to the public in July 1863 and was extended to Pembroke Dock in August 1864. For the first few years to travel from Tenby to London you had to catch the train from Tenby to Pembroke Dock, cross the Haven by Ferry to Neyland and then go to Haverfordwest and then east to London. The line was extended from Tenby to Whitland in February 1867. There were two

stops in the parish, the main station at Manorbier, with a halt at Beavers Hill, and a guarded crossing at Manorbier Newton. An additional platform was added for Lydstep (beyond Bubbleton Farm outside the parish) in 1874 to make it easier for tourists to visit the Lydstep Caverns. There had to be at least six people wanting to use the Halt or the train would not stop. A horse drawn carriage would meet the visitors at the Lydstep Halt and take them to the Caverns. In the cottage in the valley above the beach lived Betsy Brinn who would show the visitors around the caves. It must have been difficult for the ladies to scramble over the rocks wearing the dresses of the period.

Manorbier Station had a signal box where the covered waiting area is now, and there was a partially cantilevered roof, glazed on one side, which was used as the waiting room. The station master had several staff working for him, including the gate keepers at the crossings. There were two gate keepers, one at the Beaver Hill crossing and one at Manorbier Newton, and they lived in small cottages near the gates. Usually, the husband worked on the railway as a track-layer, and his wife opened the gates and operated the signal for the train. This system continued until after the Second World War, although the Lydstep Halt went out of use much earlier.

# THE GENTRY AND THEIR HOUSES

During the eighteenth and nineteenth centuries, with the County becoming more accessible, several large houses were built. The first of these was Sunny Hill off the Ridgeway for a Mr. William Byam, whose father had made money from sugar plantations in Antigua. It was built in the late eighteenth century and was owned by the family for several years. There were twelve acres of meadow land, three parlours, a drawing room and two large bedrooms, with the kitchen and various room for the servants. Outside, were stables, a brew house, a walled garden and a pleasure garden with pond. In 1851 it was being used by Miss Higgon, a school mistress from Haverfordwest, who had six boarders, four of them children, all being taught by her. The house was owned by various people until it became a farm at the beginning of the twentieth century (*Plate 11*).

Lt. John Tudor, from a Tenby family, joined the Navy at thirteen and served during the Napoleonic Wars on *H.M.S. Reindeer* in the West Indies. This ship was very successful, and during her four years on station she captured, sometimes with other ships, about twenty enemy ships. The prize money that Lt. Tudor earned made him a rich man and he left the Navy in 1809 at the age of 27 and retired to Jameston.

*An early photograph of Tudor Lodge, Jameston*

He bought several properties around the area, and lived at Walker's Cottage which he enlarged and is now known as the Tudor Lodge Inn. There were 50 acres of land with the house and it was farmed by Rev. John Harrington after his retirement as pastor of Penuel Church.

Mr. and Mrs. J. P. Adams of Holyland built Lydstep House around 1810 and used it as a seaside villa. After their death the house was let to several people. The Adams family sold in 1891 but the new owner only kept it for two years.

Mr. John Wynford Philipps came to live at Lydstep Haven in 1893. He was the eldest son of the 12th Baronet of Picton Castle, Sir James Erasmus Philipps, and was by far the most important man in the Parish, becoming later the Lord Lieutenant of Pembrokeshire. His father had inherited the baronetcy, but not the Picton Castle Estate, which was left by Lord Milford to a distant cousin. John Wynford Philipps began to restore the fortunes of their branch of the family by marrying an heiress, Leonora Gerstenberg. He became a very successful business man, investing in Latin American railways and also in cement manufacture in Britain, being instrumental in the success of the British Portland Cement Co. He was a member of Parliament for a Scottish constituency, but resigned his seat in 1894, after he had bought Lydstep House. A great supporter of Lloyd George, he wanted a seat in Wales, which he obtained when he became Liberal Member of Parliament for Pembrokeshire in a by-election in 1898. He purchased Roch Castle around 1900. He resigned from his Pembrokeshire seat due to ill health in 1908 and was created Baron St. Davids, and in 1918, he was further honoured when he was made Viscount St. Davids.

They had two sons. The first, Colwyn, was educated at Eton and Sandhurst, and became a professional soldier, receiving his commission into the Royal Horse Guards in 1908. He was a Captain by the outbreak of the First World War. His younger brother, Roland was educated at Winchester and New College, Oxford. He was an important early member of the Boy Scouts and troops were formed at Lydstep and Penally. He was Commissioner for East London and was expected to be the next Chief Scout.

John Philipps altered and enlarged Lydstep House and the inside of the house has some fine Arts and Crafts details, with heavily carved timber chimneypieces, a fine staircase and linenfold panelling. A new drive was constructed and houses were built in Lydstep village to accommodate workmen and servants. The couple were benefactors to the village and as part of their wish to improve their workers, a new reading room was built, which is now Lavender Cottage. The Quarry Inn was closed down in 1906 in an attempt to prevent people 'drinking their wages', and a Temperance Hotel was in the village in 1910, but it is not known how long it survived.

His wife, Lady Nora, was a considerable figure in her own right. She was a strong supporter of women's rights at a time when women were not enfranchised. The mainspring of the South Wales Nursing Association, which was formed to train girls to be nurses and mid-wives, Lady Nora was also said to be the founder of the Women's Institute. In 1909, she formed a Village Society for the villages of Manorbier, Penally and St. Florence, with Gumfreston joining four years later. The Society published nine editions of *Our Village Society Chronicle*, beginning in January 1913 and ending in June 1915.

The Society organised Garden Fêtes and started Choral and Dramatic Societies. The Fêtes held competitions for horticulture and home excellence. School children were given geraniums to tend, with prizes for the best blooms; Teddy Johns of Manorbier village remembered winning half a crown with his plant. There were stalls for home produced products, running races on the beach, and other stalls and entertainments. The Village Society also organised various classes in the villages and a Voluntary Aid Detachment of the Red Cross was formed and met in the newly built Parish Hall in Manorbier. Lady Nora thought that the Society would have failed utterly if "weeds and thistles were not banished from every garden, and flowers should pour forth over the grey bareness of their garden walls."

Every Christmas, she gave a party for all the children of the Parish, and a large Christmas tree would be erected in the library, with hundreds of presents underneath. The children walked around wide eyed and were allowed to choose their gifts. She also gave beef and cake for the poor families in the parish so that they could have a good Christmas feed. On wet days, Lady St. Davids would have the thirty-odd schoolchildren from Lydstep taken to and from school in a covered wagon.

It was a tragedy for the family and the parish when Lady Nora St. Davids, after an operation, died in March 1915 at the age of 55.

*Lady Nora St. Davids*

She was buried at Roch Church, with a later memorial service held on Good Friday in Lydstep Reading Room. Her younger son, Captain Roland Phillips conducted the service. Both of her sons were on leave for the funeral. With her death, a lot of her good works ended in the parish and the *'Village Society'* was no longer published.

In addition to the North Lodge and the South Lodge of Lydstep House, there was another, the Ridgeway Lodge, where pheasants were reared and released for shoots on the moors. Lord St. Davids kept Shire horses in the fields near Ridgeway Lodge and stables were built for them. George Twigg, the blacksmith at Lydstep, said that the heaviest work he ever did was shoeing a Shire stallion which "weighed about a ton, and was as big as a castle," for which Lord St. Davids had paid one thousand guineas. The West Lodge was built in 1912 in the Arts and Crafts style, the architects were M. H. Bailey Scott & E. Beresford. The new Lodge did not please everyone, the *Tenby Observer* reported that it evoked severe criticism locally, and even the designers complained, years later, that it was not built precisely as they had envisaged. Lord St. David's "considered an umbrella better than a mackintosh" and replaced copings with bargeboards and did not colourwash the house as planned, and had finished up with "flimsy picturesque associated with a cuckoo clock." Harsh words for an attractive building at the top of the lane going down to Lydstep headland.

The Croft in Manorbier was built by Thomas Hughes of Hill Farm in 1879. The property was let out to two separate families, with servants quarters at the rear.

The Barclay family originally came to the Croft for the summer season. They had a connection with Manorbier as, after Henry Barclay's father James died, his widow married Lt. Col. Ferrior, who owned property in Manorbier, including East Moor Farm. Henry Barclay was born in Weston super Mare and had served in the Crimean War as a captain in the 63rd Regiment. This regiment fought with great dis-

tinction at the Battle of Inkerman in 1864, defeating a numerically superior Russian force (*Plate 14*).

In 1876, when he was about 47 years old, he married the 26-year-old Agnes Hermione Jennings of Gellideg in Carmarthenshire. They lived at 10, The Croft, Tenby, where all their children were born. They moved back to Weston-super-Mare about ten years later, when one of their children was ill and needed specialist treatment. His wife was an accomplished horse-woman, who could drive a coach and four with skill and verve. For their visits to Manorbier they brought a full retinue of servants, butler, cook, groom, footmen and housemaids.

Mrs. Barclay was the first lady to be seen driving a car in the village. A skilled and talented wood-carver, she crafted the reredos behind the altar in St. James Church, and also the font cover, a settle and two hymn boards. Their eldest son, Fergusson Barclay, an architect, designed the reredos and font cover for his mother. Hilda Hughes of Hill Farm remembered that he was engaged to be married to Amy Holland, from near their Weston home. The banns had been published and presents had arrived when the bride-to-be changed her mind after meeting one of the other brothers, cancelled the wedding and later married him.

This is unlikely, as Amy had known all the brothers since childhood. She told her great nephew, John Thomas-Ferrand, that Fergusson changed his mind, and his brother, Herbert, who was very fond of her, proposed. Amy thought that he might be doing that to preserve the honour of the family, and told him to wait a year, and if he still felt the same way, to propose again. This he did, and they married in 1913 and lived in Weston-super-Mare, where he was a well respected lawyer. Fergusson remained unmarried.

The only daughter, Hermione, married John Loftus Adams of Holyland in 1910. The second son, Charles Barclay, farmed at East Moor after his father. He had studied farming at Norchard and is recorded as a boarder there in the 1901 Census.

Henry Barclay and his wife moved to Elm Grove in St. Florence where he died in 1912. Mrs. Barclay died in 1925, and was buried with her husband in Manorbier churchyard. There are memorials to both of them in the Church.

# THE ENTREPRENEURS

Robert Greenish, from Cleggar Park, Lamphey, built the large house in Manorbier called Glan-y-Môr in 1864. Together with John Dawkins, he founded 'Greenish and Dawkins', the Haverfordwest drapers of Commerce House in Market Street in 1849 (Commerce House has recently been rebuilt behind the original façade). He travelled to work on the newly constructed railway, catching the ferry from Hobbs Point to Neyland. He was a stickler for time, so one day when the train from Manorbier left three minutes early and he missed it, he sued the railway company and won. After that, the company altered the regulations so that they could no longer be held responsible for inexact time-keeping. Robert Greenish married Anne Maria Barber, the daughter of a naval officer. She was musically gifted and in 1865, she undertook the supervision of the music in St. James Church. To begin with, Mrs. Greenish accompanied the choir on a harmonium, and when her husband donated an organ to the Church she became the organist.

Three young sisters, Floss, Maud and Ann Isitt, from London stayed at Glan-y-Môr in the summer of 1880. Their letters describe how they went to an Eisteddfod in Tenby, and went sailing with two of the Greenish boys several times. On one occasion the sea became very rough with waves coming over the deck and the yacht kept diving up and down. Floss said that she was initially very frightened, but after a while, she thoroughly enjoyed it. Maud describes how, after a wet day the evening was fine, and they and the

Greenish children walked around the garden, had a game of touch and 'frivolled'. Afterwards it was music for the rest of the evening. She said that they liked everyone at Glan-y-Môr very much, with Mr. and Mrs. Greenish being a splendid couple, and May, their daughter, was very nice indeed and the whole family had made them all welcome.

With May's marriage to William Parcell, we come across another of the influential families in the Manorbier area. The Parcell's were farmers in South Pembrokeshire for many years, and George Parcell was the first to farm in Lydstep, when he took the tenancy of Lydstep Farm, just outside the parish, in 1800. His grandson, William, was born in 1842 and he became one of the pioneers of the Assam tea plantations, going there in 1860, just three years after the Indian Mutiny. He became one of the most important figures in the tea industry and was actively involved for over twenty years. As a sideline, he apparently trained elephants. He was 40 when he married the 21-year-old May Greenish, on 3rd October 1882.

The marriage was the occasion of great celebration in the village. The *Tenby Observer* reported: "Arches of flowers decorated the streets, flags fluttered in the breeze from the top of the Church tower, from the ancient Castle walls and from flag staffs in several parts of the village. Altogether Manorbere put on its best appearance, and the day being gloriously fine, hundreds of persons streamed into the village to take part in the proceedings."

*The wedding of William Parcell and May Greenish, 3rd October 1882*

One of the local traditions was that when the newlyweds were coming down from the Church a rope was put across the road at the bottom of the hill and the couple had to pay a small ransom before they were allowed to proceed.

After the wedding breakfast, the villagers were entertained at Glan-y-Môr, and received the thanks of the Bride and Bridegroom for their very handsome gift of silver tea kettle, cake basket and tea caddy.

Mr. John Thomas, postmaster of Manorbier, who was deputed to make the presentation, gave an address, he "expressed appreciation of the merits of your honoured parents . . ." Mr. Greenish, he said had "always shown himself ready and willing to assist with his time and purse every object for the good of the Parish." He spoke of the improvement of the village ". . . by the erection of substantial dwelling houses for the well-to-do,while at the same time the amelioration of the cottager and artisan has not been lost sight of. In the person of your esteemed mother, the sickbed of the poor have been made cheerful by her presence and her kindly disposition felt wherever she went."

The bride's wedding day jewellery included a massive silver bracelet presented to her by members of the Glan-y-Môr Clothing Club, a club for the poor, started and maintained "at her sole expense" by Mrs. Greenish.

The couple spent the first two years of their marriage at William's Tea plantation in India. When they returned to Manorbier two years later, Robert Greenish bought Fernley Lodge and gave it to them as a late wedding present. Mr. and Mrs. Parcell brought with them some of their native servants and it was said that these servants used to sleep outside their bedroom door at night to make sure that Mr. and Mrs. Parcell were not attacked "in this dangerous new country."

Anne Greenish died after a long illness in 1888 and Robert died in 1900. According to the Church Magazine: "he was seized with paralysis while handling a parting gift from his late tenant, Captain D. A. N. Lomax, of the Welsh Regiment, whose death in the Battle of Driefouteen had been announced that day." There is a memorial plaque and a stained glass window in the Church for Captain Lomax.

After the death of Robert Greenish, Glan-y-Môr was let out until after the First World War. The tenant in 1906 was Captain Charles Hunter, who was then Adjutant of the Pembrokeshire Yeomanry. His Regiment was the 4th Dragoon Guards, and he was a very keen Polo player and had several horses in stables around Manorbier. He survived the First World War, retiring as a Lt. Col. in 1924. Other tenants just before the War began were the three children, a son and two daughters, of a previous Bishop of St. David's, Basil Jones. His son was also called Basil Jones.

William Parcell and his wife became, in their turn, benefactors of the village. He was a prominent public man in the County, being a member of the County Council, a J.P. and chairman of Pembroke Town Council. Mrs. Parcell had inherited the family musical talent, and she became organist at the church, after her mother. Mr. Parcell had plans for further improvements to the village. He wanted to buy the Mill and the Mill House from the Picton Estate, renovate the house, convert the barn to a cottage for the family nanny who was about to retire and use the mill to generate electricity for the village. This ambitious idea failed, as the owners refused to sell, and the place rapidly became a ruin. One of their sons, Norman, went to Cambridge, and during one of the vacations, brought back to Fernley Lodge his fellow student, Percy Rigby. Six years later, after being appointed Vicar of Manorbier, by Christ's College, Percy married Norman's sister Marjorie, in October 1914, just after the beginning of the First World War.

*The wedding of the Rev. Percy Rigby and Miss Marjorie Parcell, October 1914*
(By permission of Mrs. June Stevenson and Squibb's Studios, Tenby)

Plate 1. *King's Quoit*

Plate 2. *Bronze Age hoard*
(By kind permission of The National Museum of Wales)

Plate 3. *Skomar Camp defences*

Plate 4. *Manorbier Castle (John Wrightson)*

Plate 5. *Lady Margaret Beaufort at prayer*

Plate 6. *Inner Court of Manorbier Castle, 1830 (H. Gastineau)*

Plate 7. *The Dovecote*

Plate 8. *Coat of Arms of William III,*
*St. James Church, Manorbier*

Plate 9. *A yeoman's cottage in Manorbier (Samuel Prout, 1830)*

Plate 10. *Norchard*
(By kind permission of Heulwen Davies)

Plate 11. *Sunny Hill. Watercolour (H. S. Burr, 1791)*
(Pembrokeshire Record Office)

Plate 12. *Park Farm, Manorbier*
(By kind permission of Sally Thomas)

Plate 13. *Lydstep Village, circa 1900*

Plate 14. *Lt. Henry Barclay (1846)*
(Courtesy of John Thomas-Ferrand)

Plate 15. *Newton Lodge, 2012*
(With thanks to Roger Minchin)

Plate 17. *Manorbier Parish Hall, 2012*

Plate 16. *Green Grove, 2012*
(With thanks to Ray Hughes)

Plate 18. *Shute Cottage, circa 2000*

Plate 19. *Manorbier Country Market, Parish Hall. Some of the stalwarts, July 2012:*
*Left to right: Helen Brickell, David Gourlay, Cheryl Hewitt, Beryl York, June Bryant, Mary Gooch, Julie Buckland, Margaret McCracken,*
*Margaret Minchin, Sam Nicholls, Pat Staley*

# FARMERS

Thomas Lewis who was the agent to the Bush Estate became guardian to Mary-Anne and Elizabeth Meyrick, two of the daughters of Sir Thomas Meyrick of Bush House, Pembroke. He married Mary-Anne and took the lease for Norchard sometime around 1835. Elizabeth Meyrick who was living with them, was courted by Benjamin Lloyd, a local farmer, who did not meet with the approval of her guardian. As she was now 37 years old, she may have thought that this was her last chance to marry, so, probably with the assistance of her sister, she absconded with Benjamin Lloyd who had a carriage waiting in the Red Lion yard in Pembroke, and they went rapidly to Bosherston where the Rev. William Bird Allen, who approved of the match, was waiting to marry them. The need for urgency was not just to make sure her guardian did not catch her, but also because marriages at that time had to be performed before noon. Apparently the marriage was a happy one and Thomas Lewis finally accepted his new brother-in-law. The Lewis family continued to hold the lease of Norchard for many years.

Francis Meyrick, one of the sons of Sir Thomas Meyrick, and brother of Mary-Anne and Elizabeth, began farming at Norchard, but then farmed at Manor Farm, Lydstep, the first of the family to farm there. The farm still belongs to his descendants.

Thomas Hughes started farming at Hill Farm in the 1860's. His son married the daughter of Francis Meyrick, and the Hughes family continued to farm at Hill Farm for over one hundred years.

The Millard family is recorded as farming at Wynd Hill in 1786 and continued there until after 1901, when the male line failed. They also farmed at Hill Farm around 1814 after James Millard married the daughter of Nathaniel Llewellyn when the male line of that family failed. They may have been farming in the Parish even longer, as the name appears in the surveys of the early 1600's.

They had a family connection to the millers at Manorbier, the Lloyd family who were at the mill for about seventy years until the 1870's. During the 1880's the miller was Eliza Grigg, the widow of a Millwright in Manorbier. The last miller at the mill was Johnny Williams, in the 1891 Census, but the mill was closed at the next census in 1901. They were also connected by marriage to the Parcells of Lydstep Farm.

By the beginning of the 20th century most of the families in the Parish were inter-related, as there was little travel outside of the Parish. Even after the Second World War, only the residents of Manorbier Newton would travel 'over the top' to St. Florence. The Twigg, Thomas, Cole, Saise and Cadwallader families are examples of marriage between local families, as are the Millards, Lloyds and Parcells and no doubt many others.

# HOUSES

Morfa Terrace, another of the Greenish family developments, was comprised of four large houses. When they were to be sold the advertisement read: "They each have three reception rooms, five bedrooms with a kitchen, wash house, larder and other conveniences, with a large garden attached. There is a separate pew for each house in the Church, which has only just been restored, about five minutes walk from the houses. Rent £46, including a first class railway pass for seven years granted to the tenant from Manorbier to Tenby or Pembroke Dock." Mr. George Greenish, son of Robert, had all four of them built. He sold no. 4 in 1878 to Edwin Minifie, whose granddaughter, Mrs. Heather Sutton, still lives there. No. 1 was sold to Mr. William Bryant in 1898, and no. 2 to Miss Jane Harries in 1893.

The Greenish family built several small houses for people living in Manorbier. The two houses of the Gables were built, as was Coglin Cottage (now Castle Cottages) and Durance Cottage (now The Boat House).

Castle Mead was originally constructed as two separate buildings, with the builders walking each day to work from Carew. They were then connected together sometime before 1871 to make a larger house. The house was let unfurnished as a desirable residence, and amongst its attractions boasted three reception rooms and nine bedrooms, a garden including a full sized tennis lawn, a stable with two stalls and a large coach house. It enjoyed two deliveries every day from the Post Office, apart from Sunday, and a regular supply of the best spring water. The occupant in the 1871 Census is Captain Verstunne, a retired Army officer, and his family.

Tarr which had been farmed by the Athoe's for many years, was burnt down around 1870, and re-built in the present

Victorian style. In 1871, it was occupied by John Grigg and his family, a Millwright.

One of the more intriguing houses in the Parish is Green Grove in Jameston. *The Buildings of Wales, Pembrokeshire*, states that old maps suggest a square moat around the site. The present house, with its projecting gable chimney, may originate from before the 18th century, but the stuccoed front with unusual raised panels is Georgian. The first reference found to Green Grove is in 1764, when the property is owned by Gwynne Davies, Esq. It is later in trust to Griffith Meyns, Esq. and in 1814 Green Grove is owned by William Hamilton Esq. Generally, at this time the majority of land-owners were not even referred to as Mr. on documents, so the implication is that the owners are a class above others. The Skyrme family farmed there during the nineteenth century. Owen Jenkins farmed at Green Grove from about 1910, after purchasing it from the previous owners. There is a strange structure built on the front of the house, with a cartouche with Owen Jenkins' initials in it and dated to 1890. It was a water tank that Owen Jenkins had built, so that his female servants would not waste time chatting around the village pump nearby. Owen Jenkins' daughter married Howard Davies, but he did not farm there, staying at his farm near Castlemartin. His son, Spencer, farmed at Green Grove after Castlemartin was requisitioned by the Army just before the Second World War. His son, another Howard, sold the house and land recently.

Some of the larger houses developed from the small stone cottages that were built during the expansion of the rural population between the mid 18th and 19th centuries. Two examples of these cottages are in Manorbier, Rose Cottage, near to the Castle Inn, and Pound Cottage, which has an extension at the rear. The original cottage at Jameston Court can be seen alongside the main road, and was extended to the rear to make a large house. The Court was owned by the Picton Estate, until the tenant, Ben Beynon, bought the farm in the 1920's. Harper's Hall was enlarged by adding to an original cottage. Harper's Land appears in the Land Tax assessment of 1831, but the name Harper appears much earlier in 1601.

# THE ARCHITECT AND THE PARISH HALL

William Arthur Smith Benson was born in 1854, the son of a barrister. He was educated at Winchester and New College, Oxford, and after military service, trained as an architect and qualified in 1880. During this time, he met Edward Burne-Jones, a major figure of the Pre-Raphaelite movement, and William Morris, the leader of the Arts and Crafts movement. Having designed furniture and metalwork for William Morris, he opened a workshop in 1880, then a factory three years later. His business expanded and his designs for fireplace accessories, light fittings and other decorative items became the fashion. His work reached iconic status and was sold in galleries throughout Europe. He then became interested in the new electrical lighting and was one of the first to advise on lighting installations. He directed the Morris & Co. furniture department from 1896, and was involved in wallpaper designs for the firm. He had married Venetia Hunt, the daughter of Alfred William Hunt, an artist and part of the Pre-Raphaelite Brotherhood, in 1886.

William Benson and his wife began taking long holidays in Manorbier in 1898, when they rented Castle Corner House (then called Manorbier House), which they bought in 1909.

The Church had started a Reading Room in Manorbier in 1901, and they decided to build a Hall which could be used as Reading Room and Parish Hall. The Church asked for public subscriptions to raise money to build the Hall, and William Benson gave a large contribution, provided he designed the building. He submitted two designs, and the chosen one was completed at the end of December, 1908, on land leased from the Picton Estate, alongside Cross House. The Parish Hall was built by Tom Davies, and the contract price was £252-5s-0d.

Designed in the classical Arts and Crafts style it was built of local limestone. Each elevation has a small Venetian window with colonnettes at a high level. There are side windows under the roof gable. The roofs meet inside in a well designed complex of beams, which enhance the interior. The high windows mean that it is not possible to see either in or out, but provide a good diffused light.

To celebrate the Hall's opening a fancy dress ball was arranged.

Over the years many dances, concerts, whist drives and other entertainments have been held there and the Hall continues in use to this day.

# POETS AND WRITERS

Manorbier had several well known writers coming down with their families to stay year after year with the same local families. The poet Walter de la Mare holidayed at Skrinkle Farm with his family. He was an adjudicator of the literary section of an Eisteddfod held at the Castle, which was organised by Lady St. Davids' Village Society.

George Bernard Shaw and his wife also used to stay, often in the Castle and a local girl could remember them both 'doddering' down to the beach. They always had a cheery word for their young friends.

Another famous writer who was inspired by the village was the novelist Virginia Woolf. She writes that the decision to be a writer occurred when she was staying in Manorbier in 1903 that "the vision came to me clearly when walking at the edge of the sea." She began 'To the Lighthouse' on another visit, whilst staying at Sea View (now Vigilant House). However, most of her writing took place at Tarr Farm, where she is said to have preferred the view.

Seigfreid Sassoon visited Walter de la Mare in 1924 after the First World War, and wrote the poem 'A Ruined Castle' inspired by Manorbier:

*The castle, built by thirteenth-century hands,*
*And weathered by six hundred years of Wales,*
*Wild, austere, and ocean-chanted, stands*
*Survivor of Time's galleon-splintering gales.*
*Postcard-attractive interest attaches*
*To veteran walls and tourists flock like*
  *sparrows,*
*Unloaded in their motor-bus-load batches,*
*Immune from boiling-lead and arrows.*
*Come wrapped in blustering wind and cloud*
  *roofed gloom,*
*To sense the blind invasions of the dead,*
*Emerging from their architectural tomb*
*To move with me by waters phosphorous-white*
*And grope through feuds and sorrows in*
  *my head.*

© Siegfried Sassoon.
(By kind permission of the Estate of George Sassoon).

# MEMORIES

## HILDA HUGHES

*Hilda Hughes holds a baguette picnicking on the beach*

Hilda Hughes, born at Hill Farm in 1899, was the daughter of Edwin and Eliza Hughes. She wrote a memoir of her life up to the beginning of the First World War. Her grandfather was Thomas Hughes, of Hill Farm, who built The Croft. She could just remember her maternal grandfather,

Francis Meyrick, of the Meyrick family of Bush, in Pembroke and who had farmed originally at the family owned estate at Norchard. Francis farmed at Manor Farm, Lydstep, and it was there that he met his wife, Emma, the Governess at Lydstep House. Hilda remembered her maternal grandmother very well, as a little lady who could speak French and German fluently. When she was six years old, Hilda had learned to whistle and was very proud of her new skill. On a visit to her grandmother, she was reminded that ladies did not whistle, and, if she would stop for the rest of the afternoon, she would get a little present. She did so and was presented with a dainty silk handkerchief, trimmed with lace, which became a very treasured possession.

Hilda describes her childhood at Hill Farm in a large family of nine children. Her mother had been a governess for the Earl of Pembroke, Hon. Sydney Herbert, near Salisbury, and her two eldest sons were named Edwin Sydney and Herbert. Emma needed help with bringing up such a large family, and the 1901 Census shows a gardener, a cook and a nurse living at the farm, together with two more farm servants. Hilda described her father as a happy jovial man who left his wife to look after her domain of the house while his was the farm. He supported his wife in the upbringing of the children and was never heard to say an unkind word to or about her. He never swore at home, or smacked or spoke angrily to his children. Edwin and his sons were teetotal and non-smokers, and no liquor was brought into the home. The only times Hilda saw her father drink was during harvest-time, when a large vat of beer was brewed for the farm workers, and her father would occasionally take a half-pint with his meal. On Christmas Eve, when a group of farm workers were 'doing the rounds' as Carol singers, they would be entertained with Christmas cake and home-brewed beer and each would be given a cash gift.

The family made their own entertainment, and Emma always found time to teach the children new games and encourage them to read and discuss books. She also taught the girls to knit, sew and do embroidery work. From a young age, Hilda always wanted to be a teacher and she would 'play school' and arrange her dolls as if they were in class, with herself as the teacher. One day at play, one of the dolls had been naughty and had to be punished. Unfortunately, 'teacher', by mistake, struck her newest doll with the cane, and cracked her face, which caused many tears.

A favourite game was called 'Family Coach' where each of the children played a part of the coach, such as horse, wheel, lamp and so on. One of the older brothers would be narrator and when your part was mentioned, you had to stand up. If you missed, you were given a forfeit, and the forfeit session ended the evening. In the summertime, as the farm was near to Presipe Bay, the children would spend many happy hours on the beach, paddling, bathing, and collecting shellfish, which would be cooked when they arrived home.

Every Sunday, the young children would go to Sunday School, and on summer evenings, with their mother, they would walk back along the cliffs with friends who would then be invited for supper. This would be a lavish spread, and afterwards they moved to the parlour for a sing-song. Her two elder brothers were choir members at St. James Church, as later were her sisters. On cold winter evenings, when it was too wet to go to Church, the children were sometimes allowed, as a special treat, to look at the many illustrated books that had belonged to their maternal grandmother. They read from their bibles taking as a chosen text one recently given by the Vicar, and discuss it. Sometimes, they would hold their own church service, with one brother being the parson, and a sister playing their own small organ.

Hilda and her sisters were members of the Girl's Friendly Society, which met on Saturday afternoon at the Vicarage, under the encouraging eye of the Vicar's wife. They used to sew and knit, read aloud from selected books, and rehearse for their concert, which was held in the Parish Hall.

The family used to be visited by Rev. E. Jenkins, the Baptist minister, for some of the servants and farmhands belonged to his church. Hilda remembers him reading 'the bumps' on her head when she was about five, and after that, he followed her school and college days with interest.

The family led an active social life, involving parties and dancing lessons in the Parish Hall for the girls, with their father escorting them there and back.

At the village school, Hilda describes the Headmaster as very stern and strict, although she felt that he always took an interest in her. Hilda enjoyed her time at Greenhill County School, Tenby, which she attended from 1912.

Hilda Hughes remembered the outbreak of the First World War, and its effect on the Parish vividly. Horses were commandeered by the dozen, and the young lads, all out for adventure and excitement, keen to do their bit, and convinced that they would only be away for a short time, collected in the village ready to sign on.

## TEDDY JOHNS

In 1985, Teddy Johns tape recorded his memories of life in the Parish. Edward Benjamin (Teddy) Johns was born in 1904 in Ashleigh House, one of the three sons of John and Hannah Johns. His father had a smallholding and the grocer's shop, whilst his mother ran the Post Office, together with a dairy and bakery. The bread was baked at 5 a.m. in a culm-

fired oven and was ready for delivery that morning. Culm was a mix of coal dust and clay, and the mix was made into balls, dried, and placed on the fire. As it was fairly difficult to start a culm fire, most people would try and keep them going, and there are tales of culm, or ball, fires kept alight for 50 years. Teddy remembered his mother saying that her culm fire had not gone out in 14 years.

His uncle, Ben Davies, owned a horse drawn haulage and taxi service in the village, and he collected supplies for the shop from Manorbier station, and flour for the bakery from Tenby Harbour. Because of the steep hill from the harbour, an extra team of horses had to be borrowed to pull the heavy wagon.

Uncle Ben had various wagons fitted out for passengers and, in a seven seater wagonette, he would pick up the holiday makers who alighted at the Lydstep halt and take them on to the Lydstep caverns. He also had a large eighteen seater four-in-hand carriage, which was used for daily sight-seeing, going from Manorbier to Stack Rocks, Bosherston, Freshwaterwest and Angle. A trumpet would sound in the village at nine o'clock to make sure all were there and the elegantly dressed visitors would set off, with picnics stowed aboard for lunch and tea. A local lad would ride on the step of the carriage to open the eighteen gates which were on the route. Teddy himself once enjoyed this privileged job.

As a young boy, Teddy went with the stonemason, Mr. Billy Lewis, who lived in Shute Cottage, to Lydstep Quarry.

He thought that they were cutting the stone for the Parish Hall. He remembered Mr. Lewis smoking his roll-ups, and persuaded him to let him try one. He was promptly sick, and then got into further trouble at home when his mother found out.

A highlight of the year was the Pembroke Fair, where as well as stalls and side-shows, young men were hired as ploughmen, waggoners, stockmen and so on, by the farmers for a year. One of the favourite games of the village boys was played where the War Memorial now stands. They would place a stone called the Dilly Duck Stone on an existing square base, and try to knock it off by throwing other stones at it. Another village 'entertainment' was when the lads from Jameston, Manorbier and Lydstep, would gather, each group in one of the three pubs. Later in the evening there would be a free-for-all between the villages, with the non-participants watching from over the hedges and cheering them on. All good fun, with perhaps a few black-eyes, but no serious damage.

Teddy earned extra money by taking drinking water from the mains tap near to the Castle entrance to the families in The Croft. He helped in his mother's shop, and would deliver milk to the houses in the village. In summertime, milk had to be delivered twice a day or it would go off in the heat. It was sold in pint and half pint measures, ladled out from a tin container.

# SOME PARISH PEOPLE

## THE BUILDER

Thomas Davies built the Parish Hall. Born at Monkton in 1859, he moved to Jameston as a young child when his father, a farm labourer, moved to the village. He trained as a carpenter with Mr. Nicholas of Carew Newton, married his daughter, and eventually became a partner in the business. Thomas Davies and his wife moved to Norton Cottage in 1890 and later to Tenby House in Manorbier, where he was in business on his own, eventually employing ten or a dozen men. He built The Glyder for his family home and moved there in about 1903. His workshop was at the back of the Glyder, and this is now a separate property, Workshop Cottage. This had building materials stored at ground level, and the workshop was on the first floor with a wood lathe and a router. The access was up a plank, with wood slats nailed on to it. Even though he had promised his wife that he would build a staircase, he never did, the only concession being to make it two planks wide when he was seventy. He also built Inglenook in 1913, on the site of the Glan-y-Môr stables. He worked with Mr. Benson on the building of the Parish Hall, and one of his apprentices remembered working at Lydstep House during his apprenticeship around 1900.

As was often the case, Tom Davies, the village carpenter, became the local undertaker. He was always known as 'Bones' Davies, partly because he was the undertaker but also because he was very thin. He built the Bier House in 1900, and used his own horse and borrowed another to pull the Bier up to the Church. The Bier is now in the museum at St. Fagan's. Polly Williams, Molly Jones's grandmother was reputedly the first person to be carried to St. James on the Bier after her early death from tuberculosis.

## BLACKSMITHS

Five generations of the Twigg family lived in Manorbier from about 1800, when Thomas Twigg farmed in Manorbier. His son, George, became a blacksmith and established his blacksmith's shop on land next door to Fernley Lodge in 1810. He was still practicing his trade in 1841, but eventually he closed the Manorbier smithy and moved to Lydstep. On the site of the original smithy, George built what was the first modern two storey house, Tenby House. He also built

three properties on Pembroke Road called Seaview, now two houses named Vigilant and Curlew Cottage, in the 1850's.

George's son, John, had opened his own blacksmith's shop in Lydstep. John was succeeded at the blacksmiths shop in Lydstep by his son, another George, who worked as a blacksmith on the construction of the Tenby to Pembroke railway in 1863. He could remember the engineer in charge of the railway, David Davies of Llandinam, Montgomeryshire, who apparently had very red eyes, and also another engineer, John Lewis of Norchard farm. George's son, yet another George, took over the smithy, which he eventually closed before moving to St. Florence in 1919. The house at Lydstep, where George Twigg lived, is still Myrtle House, and the smithy, Rose Cottage.

There was a Smithy in Jameston in 1871 run by John Watkins, and it continued until 1920, when it was eventually sold.

## POST OFFICES AND POSTMEN

The first Post Office in the Parish was in Manorbier, possibly Ashleigh House. It is first mentioned in the 1871 Census with John Thomas, a 29-year-old boot maker, who was also the Postmaster. Ten years later he was a grocer, and continued as Postmaster until his death in 1895. He was very well respected in the village. We have come across him earlier, presenting the gifts from the village to the new bride of William Parcell in 1882.

Every morning, the Post would be collected by wheelbarrow from the station where it had been left by an early train. It was then sorted at the Post Office and delivered by two postmen, one full-time, who walked about 16 miles a day, and the other part-time, who, after his morning round, would go gardening for the large houses. In the evening, the Post would be taken to the station to catch the mail train, and the wheelbarrow left there for the next day. After John Thomas' death, his niece Hannah, Teddy Johns' mother, took over. After Mrs. Johns dislocated her hip, her sister, Miss Elizabeth Davies, became Postmistress in 1910, and she ran it with their sister Ellen on the opposite side of the road, now Beach Break Tea Rooms. In 1935, the Post Office was bought by Mr. Bampkin, a postman from Saundersfoot. He moved the Office to Sea View, now part of Vigilant House, on Pembroke Road. The Post Office stayed there for a long time before moving to its present position at Gable Cottage.

There was a Sub-Post Office in Lydstep, first at the Temperance Hotel, now the Lydstep Tavern, run by Mr. Henry Fair in 1910. He was succeeded by Mrs. Alice Roberts and her husband and Mrs. Roberts was Sub-Postmistress for several years., and she moved the Post Office next door to the Reading Room, now Lavender Cottage. Mr. Thomas Spencer was the Sub-Postmaster in 1923, and also had a restaurant, perhaps back in the old Temperance Hotel building.

## PUBS AND PUBLICANS

Jameston Fair, known as Jameston Green, was held every year in July and was not a hiring or animal fair, but was for the entertainment of the locals, with travelling fiddlers, bran tubs, skittles and other amusements. The Beerhouse Act of 1830, which was intended to wean the population off more alcoholic drinks such as gin, made it easy to set up and brew and sell beer. At Fair time, some of the Jameston houses sold beer, and eventually Plough Cottage became the Plough Inn and Elm House became the Black Horse. There were other beerhouses in Jameston, one near Green Grove, and one called The Royal William which may have been opposite the Plough Inn. The New Inn which had been in the village since 1810 seems to have been renamed the Railway Inn after the railway arrived in in 1863; it then became the Swan Lake in 1935. It was, until recently, the only Public House remaining in the village.

There was a Beer House on the Ridgeway which became Jenny Kibble's pub, to the east of the turning to Manorbier Newton.

Lydstep had the Quarry Inn, which was sometime called the Quarry Hotel. It is first recorded in the 1851 Census, when it was being run by John Twigg, and he continued until 1878, when Andrew Nicholl became Publican. It was closed by Lord St. Davids in 1906. In a Trade Directory of 1910, a Temperance Hotel is listed, with the Sub-Postmaster keeping it. The Temperance Hotel no longer existed in 1923, and it was not until 1974, when the Lydstep Tavern opened on the site of the Quarry Hotel, that Lydstep had a Public House again.

There was a pub in Manorbier called The Old Castle which first appears in the 1861 Census, run by John Saise, a tailor, but it had disappeared by the 1901 Census. John Saise had married Elizabeth Twigg, of the family at the Castle Inn. The pub was on the island where the Parish Hall was later built and is now a private house called Cross House. It could have been given its name because it stood on the site of the motte, or old castle, which may have been built before the present Castle. Simon Hughes, a shoemaker, had a pub which began to trade in about 1795 called The Boot and Shoe. In the 1851 Census the Lion Inn appears, being run by John Hughes, who was also a shoemaker. Somewhere between 1861 and 1871 the Lion Inn was taken over by William Matthews, a gardener, and it was known as the Lion Hotel in the 1881 Census and was still a hotel in the 1901 Census, although Mrs. Matthews was now in charge. In 1916 Fred and Agnes Gay took it over until 1931, when they did not renew the License. It is now a block of flats called Lion House.

The Castle Inn first appears in the 1851 Census being run by Francis Twigg, who had worked for his father, the blacksmith in Manorbier. By 1881 Thomas Twigg, his son, was in charge of the Castle Inn, and ten years later his sisters, Anne and Jane, were running the pub with their brother's help. From 1914 until his death in 1954, the landlord was William Morse, and his wife continued as Licensee until 1962. The pub is still here in 2012 under the care of the Maytum family.

# THE PARISH GOES TO WAR

Prior to the outbreak of War in August 1914, a Women's Voluntary Aid Detachment (Pembroke No. 6), had been formed in the Parish, with a Men's "Bearer Squad" attached. Both were commanded by Mrs. May Parcell of Fernley Lodge.

It was reported in the *Village Society Chronicle* of May 1914 that an inspection was made by Major Jones of the R.A.M.C. The Parish Hall had been converted into a temporary hospital with eight beds, together with eight volunteer patients. As part of the inspection, the nurses were given sealed orders opened by the Lady Superintendent, Miss Hewat, and had to dress a wound, bandage a fracture, or whatever was given to them. The men's section was also examined in stretcher drill, and First Aid. The Major inspected the kitchen, their equipment and the books of the detachment, produced by the quartermaster, Miss Parcell (soon to be Mrs. Rigby).

He gave a very good report on their work, training and discipline. The members of the detachment were Mrs. Mansel, Davies, Beynon, Packer and Jensen; Misses Hughes, Benbow, C. & L. Protheroe, Thomas, Basil Jones, Richards, Evans, Warlow, Stern and Mansell. The cooks were Mrs. Evans and Scourfield, Misses Harries and Ingram, with the Bearer Squad comprising Messrs. I. Davies, Jensen, Morgan, Parcell, Teasdale and Watkins.

A later examination on First Aid by Dr. Drake shows that most of the above qualified for their certificates, and some members of the Lydstep Boy Scout troop were also examined. Willie and Fred Harries, Jack Jones and Jim Brace were awarded their ambulance badge.

In August 1914, there were about six hundred men, women and children living in the parish. Of this number, one hundred and eighteen fought in the War and twenty-eight were killed in action or died of wounds.

The two sons of Lord St. Davids of Lydstep Haven were both killed in France. Colwyn Philipps, who was a Captain in the Royal Horse Guards, was among the first British troops to arrive in France. Originally expecting to be involved in glorious cavalry charges, he soon came to realise that the war was to be a static one, and would last much longer than had been thought. He was killed in action during the second battle of Ypres, two months after his mother died on 13th May 1915. He has gained a reputation for his poetry. His younger brother, Roland was working for his father's South American railway before the war, and was a keen Scout, being responsible for Scouting in East London in 1913. He had been awarded the Military Cross on 14th April 1916 for conspicuous gallantry. "Even though he was severely wounded, he kept his men well in hand, himself killing four of the enemy with his revolver. He stuck to his post and repelled three attacks." He was killed in action on the Somme on 7th July 1916.

The four sons of the Barclay family served during the War. Herbert Barclay was one of the first men from Manorbier to volunteer. Ronald may have served in Africa, as he emigrated to Rhodesia after the war. Charles joined the Pembrokeshire Yeomanry, and finished the War with the rank of Major. Captain Fergusson Barclay was commissioned in the Somerset Light Infantry at the outbreak of war. He then volunteered for the R.F.C. (later the R.A.F.) but was seriously injured in an air crash and died three weeks after the Armistice. He was 47 years old at the time of his death.

Another villager, W. Basil Jones was also killed in 1918. A Captain in the R.A.F., he was the son of the former Bishop of St. Davids, Basil Jones, and had lived with his sisters in Glan-y-Môr.

Percy and Norman Parcell served during the War. Percy had already fought in South Africa during the Boer War and he survived the Great War. His brother Norman had become a priest, and he served as a stretcher bearer before coming back to replace his brother-in-law, Percy Rigby as Vicar of St. James.

Percy Rigby, who had married about two months after the outbreak of war, stayed as Vicar of St. James until March 1917, when he went to the front as a Chaplain to the Forces. After the War, he returned to St. James.

Lloyd Davies, the son of Tom Davies, the builder, was already in the Merchant Navy, on the *Edinburgh*.

This ship was captured by a German raider in January 1916 and then sunk, the crew having been transferred to the raider. They were then taken to South America, where they were put on another ship which took them to Tenerife, and they eventually reached home. Lloyd Davies then joined *Galgorm Castle*, where he was Third Mate. This ship, a four masted barque of 1500 tons, was in March 1917, surprised by a German submarine about 100 miles from the coast

*Lloyd Davies*

of Ireland. It was sunk by shelling, after the Germans had ordered the crew to take to the boats.

Two boats were launched one with the Captain, his wife and ten men, the other with the Mate, Third Mate Lloyd Davies and ten others. The first boat was picked up by a steamer after a day adrift, and taken to Cork. The second boat capsized in a squall, and they lost four men, the rudder and all the gear. Unable to do anything and in extremely cold and wet conditions, the men began to die and the boat was picked up with only one survivor, a Russian seaman.

Hilda Hughes' elder brother, Francis (Frank), joined up in 1916 and went to France with his Regiment. He was wounded in battle a year later at Pilkem Ridge in July 1917. He lay wounded on the field for some time before being rescued and was treated at several hospitals before being discharged in 1919. Henry Hughes, who was killed in France in 1917, does not appear to have been a relative. He was born in Ludchurch, had married and was living in Lydstep when war broke out.

Fred Johns, Teddy's brother, who was only 16 at the time War began, volunteered for the Army. His mother was very upset, as he was too young and should have been discharged. However, she spoke to Major Barclay, then a Lieutenant in the Pembrokeshire Yeomanry, who reassured her by saying he would look after her son, so she allowed him to go. He never saw the Major after he joined. They were in different Regiments. Fred served in Egypt, Turkey and Cyprus and came home after the war was over. Teddy himself, when he was thirteen in 1917, joined the training ship *Foudroyant* at Falmouth with about twenty other boys. This ship had been purchased by G. Wheatly Cobb, the son of Joseph R. Cobb, who had restored Manorbier Castle.

Two of the three sons of William and Emma Johns, of Ash (then known as Tin) Cottage, Manorbier, did not survive the war. Wilfred was killed in action in France in May 1915, and his brother Bertie killed in Mesopotamia (now Iraq) in December 1916.

Joseph Harrington had been the Baptist Minister of Jameston before war began. He and his wife Kezia lived in Tudor Lodge where he farmed fifty acres. Three of his sons volunteered. Two of them had emigrated to Western Australia, and they were in the 16th Battalion Australian Infantry. The eldest, William, died of his wounds in May 1917 aged 33 in a prisoner of war camp. His 23-year-old brother, Reginald, died only three months later in August 1917.

Two other brothers, Charles and William Allen, sons of William and Frances Allen of Milton Cottage, Manorbier, were also killed. They volunteered straight away, and Charles died in France in December 1914. His brother was living in London when he enlisted, and he was killed in France in July 1917.

Sixteen other men from the Parish were killed, mostly in France or Flanders. Two villagers died in the Middle East. Lieutenant Frederick Bryant, whose parents lived in Morfa Terrace, lost his life in March 1917 as did Benjamin Scourfield of Gable Cottage, Manorbier, in November 1917. Two men were serving in the Royal Navy when they were killed: William Shipley in 1914 and George Bush in October 1918. George Rixon died of wounds on board a hospital ship after being wounded while fighting in the Dardanelles.

Two others died of their wounds after the fighting had ended, Frederick Thomas in December 1919 and William Williams in September 1920. Mrs. Thomas, who worked as a teacher at the school, is recorded in the school log being away on the afternoon of 28th September 1916 as her husband was home on his last leave before going to the front. Later, on 10th May 1918, she is away with the Manager's permission and has gone to London to visit her husband who is in hospital wounded. He was released from hospital but never fully recovered and died a few years later.

Here follows an extract from a letter written by Colwyn Erasmus Arnold Philipps, Captain Royal Horse Guards, to his brother Roland, who was still in training in England, giving advice on survival in the French trenches. The letter is dated November 27th, 1914:

"... All officers should know how to stop an artery in any part. As there can be no appliances and it is often impossible to move, little first aid can be done, but iodine and stopping bleeding are essential, I advise all to carry some pain-deadening pills, as a man screaming will shake a company's nerves more than shells. However bad a man may be never allow him to be taken from the trench by daylight unless he can be moved under cover. It is absolutely wrong to risk sound men if it can be avoided by waiting until dusk.

Usually the men are lazy about digging at first, but after a little shelling they are all the other way, and it is most important that you prevent them digging the trench so deep that they can't fire out of it. There is some doubt as to the best way of meeting an attack, some still advising the men to get out of the trench and meet it with a bayonet. I think these are the people who have not tried getting out of a trench in a hurry; the men get out at different times, some one side, some the other. If they know for certain that they will never get the order to get out, they will continue to shoot steadily until the last moment. As a matter of fact, you have lots of time to get out when the Germans get in, as they are very bad hand-to-hand, and always attack at night, so if you have to run they don't usually hit many, and they never pursue. Always carry lots of ammunition to the trenches: you may not want it for months, but when you do you will find 200 rounds don't go far. You will usually take over trenches at night; don't in the confusion forget to ask the chap you relieve:

Where the supporting trench is.
Exactly who is on your flanks, and where.
Where the dressing station is.
If any water is to hand, and where.
If you have wire in front of you; and if you have not, you must have half of the men standing to arms all night.
If you hear tremendous fusilades going on it will probably be yeomen or French: don't stand to arms without real need. A good regiment will be in the trenches for days and hardly fire a shot, a bad one will have bursts of rapid once an hour.

Well old boy, I wish you every kind of luck. Another hint – Do not, however great the temptation, allow straw in the firing trenches (have it in the supports of course) nothing gives the show away so. The other day I found my trench lined with nice warm straw pallets. We were shelled like hell, but in the night I had all the straw carried out and put in a line 200 yards behind us. They shelled this line of straw all day and never touched us.

We are still resting. I believe the real reason is that both sides have run out of big gun ammunition. I'm awfully glad you are doing so well, old boy; who knows, the . . . and the . . . may bring off one of these stirring charges the papers talk about, but which have never happened."

Colwyn was gazetted to the Scots Guards on May 15th, two days after he fell in action in a charge of the Royal Horse Guards near Ypres, 13th May 1915.

A small detachment of troops were stationed in Manorbier Castle during the early part of the war. When they left in 1915, the *Village Chronicle* noted that: "it is with genuine regret on both sides that we parted with these men who have won the goodwill of everyone in the village. May good luck attend them whether here or at the front." There are tales that these young soldiers were spooked by the silence of the countryside. One of them, left for a short time on guard on his own, was approached by a lady dressed in white. When she ignored him and came on, he fired at her and the bullet passed straight through her, and she then vanished. At that, the guard panicked and knocked himself out while trying to run away.

A Coast Watch was formed in the Parish to look out for any enemy shipping. These were men who were no longer young enough to join the forces.

They are, from the left, Mr. James Faithful, Mr. Tom Davies, Mr. Morse of Jameston, Capt. James, Mr. Billy Lewis of Shute Cottage, and Mr. Bill Harries, who was a shoemaker.

Life went on in the Parish even though most of the young men had gone to war. Mrs. Rigby, the vicar's wife, was a V.A.D. nurse at the Military Hospital at Pembroke Dock, and organised concerts in the Parish Hall to raise money for the war effort.

On New Year's Eve 1915 the *SS Satrap*, a collier from Newport, was lost with all hands off Manorbier during a heavy gale. Three unidentified members of the crew were buried in St. James churchyard. There is a brass plaque in the Church given by Mr. Pardoe Thomas and the Trident Line, the owners, thanking the people of Manorbier for their support.

At Manorbier school, the children were regularly given news on the progress of the war. They were given a half day off when Jerusalem was captured from the Turks in December 1917. Three days after the naval battle of Jutland on 3rd June 1916 Lord Kitchener drowned when his ship was torpedoed. The pupils were given a lecture on his life. All the children were given 'Peace Mugs' when the war was declared over in 1919.

A strange postscript to the war happened when a dead whale was washed up on Manorbier beach in April 1919. Thought to have been killed by a mine the whale caused a lot of interest and many people visited Manorbier to see it. According to Mrs. Rigby, it was a Narwhal, which is a subspecies of whale with a tusk and is normally found in Arctic waters. Mr. William Parcell, her father, cut off the tusk and a team from Cardiff took the skeleton to the museum.

Unfortunately, the remains were left on the beach, with a smell that got stronger each day. It was still there twelve months later but the novelty value had worn off. Eventually, the tide took the remains away and with them went the smell.

# BETWEEN THE WARS

At the end of the War, Pembrokeshire County Council purchased East Moor, Calvesland and Cow Park farms, which were then split into several small-holdings, and let to ex-servicemen. Although men survived the war many had been damaged. Some suffered from the lingering effects of mustard gas attacks, as had Ernie Rees, whose father had purchased Newton Lodge Farm after the war. He continued to farm but was unable to do all of the heavy work.

Lord St. Davids and his second wife sold Lydstep Haven in 1926 to the Earl of Essex, who owned the only aeroplane in Pembrokeshire at the time. The aeroplane was most likely a De Havilland Gypsy Moth, a two seater plane which had a luggage compartment large enough to take a set of golf clubs. It was kept in a large metal shed near to Honey-suckle Lodge by the railway line.

Charles Barclay still lived at the Croft. He married, aged 45, Nesta Lloyd of Glangwili in Carmarthenshire, who was 20. The couple moved to Morfa Terrace in 1927. Major Charles Barclay was the first person in the village to have a telephone, and a petition was got up by the villagers to persuade him not to install it. However, when it was up and running, everyone wanted to use it! While they lived in Manorbier he was a Churchwarden at St. James Church and, after moving to St. Florence in 1930, they were still involved with the village and are both buried in the new graveyard.

Charles Barclay's sister, Hermione Adams, lived with her husband, Major John Loftus Adams, at Tarr Farm after the First World War. They had previously lived at East Moor after they were married. Her husband had fought in the War with the Pembrokeshire Yeomanry. They had one son and two daughters. Their son, John, had a passion for ships and engines, and used to go to Milford Haven when young to help on the trawlers. They left Manorbier about ten years after the War, and moved to the family home, Holyland, near Pembroke. John joined the Merchant Navy and travelled the world on several ships.

In 1920, Glan-y-Môr was sold to Margaret Simon, the Aunt of Lord Simon who was variously Home Secretary, Chancellor of the Exchequer and so forth to successive governments. He famously fell out with Lloyd George during the First World War and was dismissed from the government. His widowed mother, Fanny, came to live with her sister-in-law, and Lord Simon would visit. Teddy Johns remembers meeting the train to pick up Lord Simon when he was being protected by armed guards, and Lord Simon insisted on travelling in Teddy's Model-T Ford taxi, with his guard following in a limousine.

William Parcell continued to live in Fernley Lodge after his wife, Marianne (May), died in 1922. A tribute was paid to her by the parishioners when, a fortnight before her death, they assembled in large numbers to hear a sermon given on the lawns of Fernley Lodge by her son, Norman. William served as a Churchwarden for over forty years.

William Parcell's daughter, Marjorie, and her husband, Percy Rigby, were living at the Vicarage (now the Old Vicarage) after his return from France. Her brother Norman, who had taken over the Parish in her husband's absence, was granted his own living at Sketty, near Swansea. Norman was a talented designer, and was involved in the design of several of St. James Church windows. He used to bring young members of his Church and the local Scouts from Sketty to Manorbier. They stayed in a hut which overlooked a small bay known locally as Water Come-on, which is between Presipe and Conegar Bays. Percy Rigby and his wife were very sporty. They played badminton, tennis and cricket, and he was President of Tenby Golf Club for over twenty years. He attended to his Church duties with diligence and enthusiasm, and is remembered fondly by the older members of the parish as 'a real gentleman'.

One of the tales told about Percy Rigby concerned Billy Lewis. When Billy was getting older, he decided to take to his bed upstairs in the loft of Shute Cottage. He was described as a lazy old rascal and it meant that his wife, who was also elderly, had to go up and down the shaky steps to look after him. The Rev. Rigby decided that he would get one of his golfing friends, Dr. Charlie Mathias, to look at him. Although an excellent doctor, he was extremely rough and ready, and outspoken. A large man, he squeezed his shoulders into the loft, looked round and said: "How the hell are we going to get the corpse out?" Billy Lewis came down that night.

Frank Hughes, when he had recovered from his wounds, found that he was no longer fit enough to do the heavy farm work. One day he was visiting the village shop, and the owner, Lizzie Codd, asked him if he wanted to take over the business. After talking to a grocer friend of his, he took a two year lease on the shop. When the lease ended, he bought the business and the six-bedroomed house for £700. His business grew as the village grew, and he had to extend the shop two or three times. He and his wife Bessie had a large family of eleven children, and they only retired from the shop after 56 years when he was 83.

Tobias and Lizzie Codd lived over the shop for a while, and one of Frank's children can remember her father telling her that the Codd's used to argue all the time. During one of their arguments, Lizzie stormed out slamming the door,

*You can just make out Teddy John's cows*

Teddy Johns supplied Manorbier with milk. His cows grazed on the field near the beach, and were driven through the village to be milked.

Miss Protheroe, from Penally, took over a shop in Jameston in 1923, which had been selling animal seed. She and her new husband, Eastlake Williams, changed it to a grocery store which they continued to run until 1962.

There had been another grocer in Jameston at Wesley House, run by William Brace in 1914, but this had closed by 1923.

A woman brought fish from Milford Haven for sale in the parish. Using the ferry, she crossed the Haven with the morning catch, caught the train to Beaver's Hill crossing, and walked around the villages selling the fish. If it was a hot day, to make sure that her fish kept, she would wash them in a stream to freshen them up.

Washerwomen collected clothes to be washed from the houses. One who was remembered, Maggie Brooks, would walk from her home at 'The Plough' in Jameston with the

saying that she had had enough and was going to jump in the sea. When she came back, her husband said: "Was the water too cold, Lizzie?"

Mrs. Johns had closed the bakery in Manorbier village, and two other bakers started making deliveries. One was from Tenby and had a horse drawn cart, but White's of Lamphey, who established their bakery in 1921, owned a motorised delivery van, and were considered very modern.

basket balanced on her head and went to the other villages to collect and deliver the washing.

There were so many rabbits that a rabbit factory existed in Pembroke, where the meat was prepared, and the skins used to make gloves and other clothing. The rabbits were trapped or netted, and taken to the station for delivery to London and other cities, and to the butcher for local consumption.

*Left to right: Unknown; Tommy Brown; Albert Brown; Charlie John; Jack Phillips*
(Photo courtesy of Keith Johnson, and reprinted here by kind permssion of Mrs. Dilys Cole)

Lydstep village had its own tramp, Freddy Thompson, who lived in a tin shack in one of the Norchard fields. He survived on casual labour and lived there all year round, having a fire in the winter which made the place very smoky.

Mrs. Rigby organised lots of entertainment in the Parish Hall. There were music and fancy dress competitions for the children and concerts for adults. The concerts featured singing, comedy and any other acts that could be found. One of the star turns was Ernest Handel Evans, nicknamed 'Micky', from Jameston, a brilliant pianist, though largely self taught. Mrs. Rigby's cousin Geoffrey Greenish was a good comedian, and another Greenish cousin, Doris, a very good violinist. Two of the singers were a Jameston resident, Wilfred Hicks and Edwin Howell, who lived at Castle Mead. Teddy Johns remembered that during one of these concerts, Tom Twigg stood up to recite a poem. The vicar felt that it was a little bit near the knuckle and Tom was given money for beer and told to go away. Dances and whist drives were also held at the hall. There was only one fire for heating, and no lavatory, but fortunately there was an earth closet behind the house next door. Mrs. Evans, the pianist's wife, made tea in a large black pot downstairs and this area was used as a changing room during the shows.

Each summer a lot of the social life revolved around the tennis courts in the village, with courts at Fernley Lodge, Glan-y-Môr, Manorbier Castle House, Castle Mead, the Croft and Castle Corner House. Now, there is only one court left at Pound Cottage.

Cricket was one of the games where all levels of Parish society played in the same team. During the twenties, the main players were Rev. Percy Rigby, Thomas Cogbill from Lydstep and Cecil Keyte of Glan-y-Môr Cottage, and they played at 1, 2 and 3 in the batting order, and did most of the bowling. Other team members were T. Johns, F. Meyrick, P. Brace, S. Thomas, P. Phillips and D. Evans among others. The team set a scoring record in the 1924 season, but it was unfortunately the lowest score as they were all out for seven runs. At least they did not lose the match, which was played over two innings, and they played out for a draw in the second innings. The cricket pitch had been originally on Norchard land, opposite the Railway Station, but it had moved to behind Fernley Lodge.

Football was always 'a gentleman's game played by ruffians' and in a description of a game played between Manorbier and Penally, this is definitely what it was. The Manorbier side had a forward line of five of the fastest runners in the area, and as the game was not then very scientific, but mainly 'kick and rush', the forward line was going fast, not taking much notice of who was in front of them, when they ran into the referee, and knocked him flying. The referee was the Rev. John Garfield Davies, later to be Vicar of St. James, Manorbier. He was not amused, and threw the Manorbier team off the pitch, and ended the game. After he had gone, the game started again, but the Vicar returned and threw them off again, not being very pleased! The football pitch was on New House (now Lime Cottage) land, between Penuel Chapel and Slough Cottage.

Another sport was running, and the Parish had three good sprinters, Tommy Scourfield and William Nicholas from Manorbier and Billy Meyrick from Lydstep. During one race, they conspired that Tommy Scourfield, who was the fastest runner, should lose, and they would all bet on the agreed winner. They said that they would get odds of 3/1, and could make a lot of money. However, Tommy Scourfield said that he did not have enough spare money to win much on betting and he would be better off winning the first prize, which he did.

In 1916 the largest and oldest bell at St. James, the Tenor bell, dated 1639, had broken away from its fixings and had fallen into the Bell chamber. Nothing could be done until the War was over, but when it ended two floors of the tower were pierced, and the bell lowered down through the tower. The bell was recast and inscribed Peace Bell, with the names of the Vicar, Percy Rigby, and the Wardens, W. G. Parcell and J. M. Collins and dated 1919. The bell was delivered to the station, and a team of horses hauled it up to the Church, where it was lifted into position in the tower causing much excitement.

The Church at Manorbier and the Mission Hall at Jameston, together with the Baptist Church at Jameston and Ebenezer Chapel at Manorbier Newton all had their Sunday schools. The two nonconformist Sunday Schools celebrated their anniversaries, with Penuel's being on New Year's Day and the Ebenezer Chapel's on Good Friday. Each child had

to perform a 'piece' which could be a poem or song, which was fairly nerve-racking in front of all the proud parents. All the Sunday schools had an outing, often driven by Teddy Johns. They may not have gone very far, sometimes to Swanlake Bay, Park Farm Valley, or Freshwater East, but they were enjoyed and remembered by all the children who went on them. Gwen Rothwell remembers going to Freshwater East for the Penuel Church outing. Gwen used to go to the Church three times on a Sunday, twice with her parents in the morning and evening, and once on her own to the Sunday School in the afternoon, walking from May Cottage, near to the Castle Inn, every time. Gwen said this afternoon visit allowed her parents to have a 'cuddle'.

There was an occasion in the mid twenties when a driver was charged with cruelty to his horses on a Sunday School trip from Tenby to Park Farm valley. He had apparently been drinking, and the witnesses, James Rixon of Jameston and William Brace of Park Farm, said that he drove the horses with the wagon attached into a ditch, and fell into the road. While trying to get the wagon out, the driver was hitting the horses and he drove them over a bank, and it took about half an hour to get them up again. The police arrested him and he was fined £3 and costs for cruelty.

The children walked to school every day and the children from Whitewell and Bubbleton walked to Manorbier as it was nearer than Penally. During break time they played in the field opposite the school, which now has holiday chalets on it.

In November 1934 there was a tragedy. Mrs. Maria Harries, the caretaker, was found floating in the water tank, having drowned. Molly Cater (later Jones) remembers that her schoolfriend, Ethel Phillips, found Mrs. Harries and was telling Molly about it when the headmaster told them to stop talking or they would be separated. Ethel put her hand up to be allowed to speak and she then told the headmaster what she had found. He probably did not believe her, but went outside to check. When he came back he got into his car to telephone for help and the children were sent home. Maria was buried in Manorbier Churchyard.

## CHANGE IN THE PARISH

It was a bad time for employment in Pembrokeshire between the Wars. The Dockyard closed at Pembroke Dock in 1924 and agriculture continued its long decline which was only ended by the Second World War.

There is still a reminder of the time when the Dockyard closed overlooking the beach in Manorbier. Because of the planned closure, the Army Camp at Llanion was being run down and one of their large huts was obtained by Mr. Brace of Park Farm in 1921 to be used as holiday chalets. It was divided into two, new ends made, and one chalet was called The Dak and the other Tranquillity.

Tranquillity was slightly further down the hill from the Dak and the remains of its garden can still be found in front of the parking spaces. The Dak was purchased by Mr. Read and Mrs. Badham and used as a café. They also provided bed and breakfast accommodation. Lloyd George visited the Dak for tea when he was in Tenby.

During the thirties, Cardiff architect, T. Alwyn Lloyd, designed two houses in the village. Long Park was built for W. A. S. Benson, the architect of the Parish Hall. He and his wife moved there from Castle Corner. In her old age Mrs. Benson was looked after by Jean Hughes (now Kitchen), until her death just before the Second World War. T. Alwyn Lloyd also designed Greenala in Mead Lane, for a Miss Taylor. Wallace Cater was her gardener and a bungalow was built for him and his sister to live in.

The Gate, next door to Withyhay, was originally a small cottage, but this caught fire in the thirties and was burnt down, and a new house was built on the site. This was the first time that a fire engine had been called to Manorbier. It did not appear to have been very successful.

Fire was a continual fear for the farmers, as hayricks would sometimes self ignite. In a letter written in the twenties, the writer, who is living in Croft House, says that a rick is on fire at Hill Farm, and another one is too close for safety. Fortunately the wind was blowing away from it, but the writer is concerned as "there is so little water up there."

A churchyard extension was needed and the land for this was given by Sir Frederick Meyrick of the Bush Estate. Work began in 1928 with the outside wall built by Tom Davies and Timothy Thomas. The churchyard needed levelling, and several villagers volunteered their services. The Vicar and Mrs. Rigby entertained the 'Church-yard Workers' Union' to dinner at Christmas at Fernley Lodge. "A very enjoyable evening was spent to which Mr. Geoffrey Greenish contrived not a little good fun. In fact all were in excellent trim, probably owing to the excellent Christmas pudding." After the Christmas holidays, work had not gone so well but a faithful few did excellent work and there was not much left to be done by March 1929.

*Back row, left to right: James Brace; Stanley Thomas; Tom Davies (carpenter); Ben Warlow (Church Cottage). Middle row: Percy Rigby (Vicar); William Brace (Park Farm); Maurice Davies (gardener); John Parr (schoolmaster). The young girls: June Rigby; Doreen Scourfield.*
*Front, seated: Marjorie Rigby; E. Howell (Castlemead); Tom Johns (Tarr Farm); E. Evans (gardener); William Scourfield (groom); David Warlow (son of Ben Warlow)*

Some of the members of the working party are shown in the photograph.

There was a shipwreck in December 1929 when *HMS Tormentor*, a destroyer, broke away from tow during a storm when she was being taken to the breakers. It was recalled by the villagers as a very rough night. The wreckage was discovered in Presipe Bay the day afterwards but nothing was ever found of the four men on board. A service was held on Priests Nose by the Vicar of Manorbier, the Rev. Percy Rigby.

Even before the war, motor vehicles had begun to take over from horse drawn vehicles for transport, and this trend accelerated as ex-Army lorries became available. The carter in Manorbier Newton did not survive the competition. After the war, motor cars became affordable to more people, and the motor-cycle, which was considerably cheaper, was even more popular.

When Teddy Johns was invalided out of the Navy, he started selling petrol to the increasing numbers of motorists in the village. In the summer of 1928, he had about two hundred cans of petrol for sale. The Johns family, who had run many horse drawn vehicles before the War, bought a Model-T Ford and started a taxi service. It was a coupe, with a canvas roof and side windows, and was sometimes used as a hearse. Not designed as one, the coffin would be tied on to the carrier at the back of the car and taken up to the church at night. A purpose built garage to sell petrol was eventually built on the site of the tennis courts of Castle Corner House, where the present garage now is.

The Omnibus was another development that offered affordable transport to reduce the isolation of the Parish. To prevent competition between the companies, Morrisons went from Manorbier to Tenby on a Saturday, and Silcox went to Pembroke from Jameston on a Friday. Even then, the last bus from Tenby would return by 6 p.m. and the last train by 7, so, if one wished to return later, the only choice was to walk home. Eventually the services improved.

With travel becoming less expensive, Manorbier became a less exclusive place. Glan-y-Môr became a hotel when it was purchased by Mr. and Mrs. Phillips, and Mr. and Mrs. Jimmy John at Fernley Lodge also started to take in paying guests, as did the Harrington sisters at Tudor Lodge. David Beynon of Picton Cottage, Thomas Scales at Baldwin's Moor and Morris John at Tarr House were all offering apartments in 1923. There was even a railway carriage converted for use as accommodation, parked in a siding at Manorbier station.

In 1924, land was purchased from the Picton Estate in Park Farm valley, and water extracted from the springs there. The water was treated in a small works and pumped up to a reservoir behind Hill Farm. This supply then came back to a tap in the wall near where the War Memorial now is, and was used by the villagers for several years. The boys in the village used to deliver water to the larger houses and charge them either a penny or a halfpenny depending on how much water they had. Some years later, a pipe was laid from the waterworks at Carew Cheriton up to the Ridgeway then down to Manorbier Newton along Haylands Lane to Jameston and along the main road to Manorbier and

Lydstep. The original water supplies in the villages, the stream at Shute Cottage for Manorbier, the village pump in Jameston and other supplies, were continued to be used by some of the villagers who did not trust 'new fangled' water.

Some of the housing in the villages was of a very poor standard. The County Council had recently been given powers to condemn houses as unfit for human habitation and they could also build houses to let to replace these properties. Two of these houses were built in Manorbier next to Inglenook and four more in Jameston at Bush Terrace. Crickmarren House next to the Swan Lake public house was demolished and the occupants re-housed in the new council houses. It had been the home of a prosperous farmer in 1786, but no longer had any land by 1814.

*Crickmarren House, Jameston*

# MILITARY MANORBIER AND THE SECOND WORLD WAR

In 1860, long before the two World Wars, Manorbier was considered as a site for a fort to protect Pembroke dockyard against a possible attack from the French Navy. This was to be put on 38 acres of land between Swanlake Bay and Manorbier Bay, and the War Department obtained the land in August 1861 to build a fort. However, they decided against one, and the only fort built in the area was on St. Catherine's Island off Tenby. The Ministry of Defence still own the land on the cliff top.

*The Times* newspaper, in November 1933, reported about a landing field near Manorbier Station for landplanes that wanted to visit Pembroke Dock RAF seaplane station. The directions for finding it were a little crude, it was described as near to the "t" in Jameston on sheet 7 of the quarter mile to one inch RAF edition of the O.S. map. The Commanding Officer at Pembroke Dock required 48 hours notice so that cattle grazing on the field could be moved before the plane landed. The C.O. also wanted to know how much fuel would be required, and it was forbidden to stay overnight unless circumstances were exceptional, as there were no facilities.

A new airfield was built in 1937 at Skrinkle, which became RAF Manorbier. There were three grass runways, to tow targets and to launch and land pilotless aircraft for use in conjunction with a proposed Gunnery training range. The first unit to move in was B Flight of No. 1 Anti-Aircraft Co-operation Unit, which was equipped, initially with Westland Wallaces, a Bi-plane, used for target towing. There were always problems with the grass runway due to flooding in the autumn and winter and, to make matters worse, the runway also dipped down in the middle. The area was eventually drained and earth moved from below Baldwins Moor Farm to raise the ground level.

The road to Skrinkle Farm, going from alongside Skrinkle Cottage was covered over, and a new road, built in its present position, lead to the Camp. A hangar was built to the west of the road, with all the associated buildings; some of them were on the field which is now used as the football pitch. The pilotless 'Queen Bees', a modified Tiger Moth, were used after target-towing aircraft were superceded. They were controlled from the ground, and the flight varied to make the gunner's task more realistic. Sometimes the

'Queen Bee' would go out of control and on one occasion, continued flying for about a hundred miles out to sea. RAF Manorbier was always separate to and outside the confines of the School of Artillery.

Because of the change in the international situation and the general fear of bombing campaigns, confirmed by the Spanish Civil War, the government developed a plan for the anti-aircraft defence of the country in 1935, which asked for a large increase in the numbers of guns, searchlights and the aircraft-detection system now known as Radar. Manorbier became involved in this plan after a visit to the area by the Western Command, who decided that it was a possible site for a practice anti-aircraft camp. Not being very complimentary to our Parish, nor to its nascent tourist industry, they reported that it was "very wild and little known to the public with a few holiday makers at the height of the season."

A School of Anti-Aircraft Artillery was opened at Old Castle Head in 1937. It was built on land commandeered mainly from Skrinkle Farm and some from Hill Farm. During the summer of 1937, the Army first appeared in Manorbier and set up a base at Skrinkle Farm, where the men lived under canvas until the Autumn. They reappeared in the Spring of 1938, camping again, but they had problems later in the year when a gale blew down most of their tents. By now, the permanent camp was being constructed and when war came in 1939 the School of Gunnery was moved from Biggin Hill in Kent to Manorbier.

Guy Gibson, who was to lead the Dam Busters and be awarded the Victoria Cross, was on holiday here in the summer of 1939. He was not very impressed by the skills of the anti-aircraft gunners. He had: "been invited by a Brigadier to attend the standard army summer game of shooting at a pilot-less aeroplane down at Manorbier. I went, and for two hours watched the army gunners fire hundreds of shells at the little biplane as it flew forwards and backwards over their heads at 500 ft. It was pretty poor shooting and it wasn't even touched. When it came in to land, it held off too long and crashed into the sea. 'We got it in the end,' said the Army officer."

At this stage the camp was nowhere near finished, with the men still having to sleep in tents, although there were buildings for the office block and mess room. The small hut which had been used by the boys from Sketty, who used to drive the local girls wild with excitement every summer they came, and by the Greenish family, overlooking Water Come-on Bay although not within the new range, had the bedding stolen and the hut damaged beyond repair. The Greenish family got £5 compensation, and the hut was demolished. A civilian chef came to cook at the camp and, after one look, he left and never came back. During construction, some of the officers and men were billeted around the Parish and in Tenby, moving out in the summer so that holiday makers, who were still coming in the early part of the war, could move in. When the Artillery School's quarters were finished, no-one wanted to move to the camp from their comfortable billets.

There were benefits to the Parish when the camp was being constructed. Work was available with a relay of carts bringing necessary materials. Gravel was taken from the beach and sand taken from the sand hills that had been deposited in the valley between the Castle and the Church during the seventeenth century. The sand was suitable to make concrete as there was hardly any salt left in it after more than three hundred years. There were two sites where the sand was being won, one run by Mr. Jimmy John, from a very large sand hill on the west side of the beach.

Mr. Ivor Mathias, had a more mechanised set-up on the east side of the beach, removing sand-hills situated below the Church. He used tubs on rail tracks to carry the sand to lorries and carts, with horses pulling the tubs back for refilling.

Tarmac was the contractor for the camp construction, and George Wimpey built runways throughout the county. From July 1940 to March 1941, when construction was at its height, George Wimpey moved 1,200 tons from the beach. Later, a Haverfordwest firm, Hussey, Egan & Pickmere, took over 400 tons during the early part of 1942. This extraction of sand continued throughout the war, with large amounts going via Manorbier station out of the county. The horses used for this work were kept at Pound Walls, and they were grazed in the field behind.

The permanent staff for the whole School eventually reached 4,500, which is about the same as the population of Tenby today, and by the end of the war, they had trained over 30,000 Allied and Home Guard officers. Among those trained was the future Prime Minister, Edward Heath, who recalled his training here when he revisited Pembrokeshire in 1973. Just after he had been commissioned, he was sent to Manorbier on the gunnery course and was told to book into one of the best hotels in Tenby. He duly did so, and caught the bus which had been laid on to take him and his fellow officers to Manorbier. On the bus, he realised that he was the only subaltern there and the other passengers were all Brigadiers. He later discovered that there were two officers courses at Manorbier, one for Brigadiers, who stayed in Tenby, and one for subalterns who stayed on the camp. He had been put on the wrong one.

Manorbier station would be closed at times as the ammunition which was needed for the School of Artillery was unloaded and transported to the Camp.

The women's branch of the Army, the ATS, fulfilled all kinds of domestic and secretarial duties at Manorbier. They lived in the 'Mae West' lines so called because of the sinuous shapes of the camouflage painted on their huts. Some of these girls were chosen to check the accuracy of the gunners using Kine-Theodolites. They had to be mathematically qualified and were nicknamed Kine-Girls. There were two Kine stations, one on the old Skrinkle Iron Age Fort, and the other towards Presipe Bay. They sighted from one station to the other as a base line, and then filmed the target, which was flying in front of the guns. The resulting film showed the explosions of the shells then, by examining the film, the accuracy of the gunners was analysed.

As well as the Gunnery Wing, the School had a Trials Wing which carried out experimental work on Lydstep Head. This comprised a complex of fifty huts, roads, hard standing and a gun emplacement.

Lydstep House had been commandeered and was surrounded by high fencing, with armed guards at the two roads down to Lydstep House. No unauthorised personnel were allowed inside, but Mr. George Mathias did once enter the secure area. One of his dogs from Norchard somehow got in the heavily guarded area, found the canteen, and proceeded to eat over a dozen of the dinners. George was summoned to catch his dog, and was taken in a covered lorry, and guarded all the time so that he could not look out. On arrival he was told to call his dog which jumped into the back of the truck and they were driven out.

The secret project at Lydstep House was to create radar-guided gunnery to improve gunfire accuracy. During the Blitz, the gunners had had to rely on search lights picking out the aircraft before firing on them. ATS Kine-girls, who had been specially chosen for this secret work, moved to the South Lodge of Lydstep House which was used as a kitchen and recreation room with a Nissen hut alongside

for their sleeping quarters. They worked with the radar experts of the Army in the library of the House.

*Kine-girls in training*

To test the various types of gun control, a mobile 3.7-inch anti-aircraft gun was used. The concrete base of this gun emplacement has survived. Six different methods of gun control were tried to ascertain which worked best. The sixth method was radar control, and in the early stages the control was so unsuccessful that the gun would perform crazy manoeuvres and swing inland and to any position other than the target. After further development, the aim of the gun improved until in October 1942 they hit the target with the radar controlled gun. Being unable to believe their success, another target plane flew over and there was another direct hit. Eventually they had four hits in a row before it began to rain and stopped them. This was the turning point and even though they were not immediately able to repeat their successes, the system was developed. These radar controlled guns were used to shoot down V-1 missiles in the later stages of the war.

There was a self-contained Radar station at Old Castle Head built after the Battle of Britain. This was used to detect low-flying aircraft and shipping in the Bristol Channel and the entrance to Milford Haven. The reinforced concrete transmitter-receiver block and the stand-by generator block can still be seen inside the camp boundary. There was a Searchlight battery training area in a field behind Wind Hill Farm which had thirteen huts, a searchlight cluster, and three weapons pits.

# FRATERNISATION

Dennis Williams earned quite a lot of money as a schoolboy delivering telegrams to the Camp. He had been attending school in Pembroke Dock and after the town was bombed, the school was closed for some time. Dennis was at home with nothing to do. He called in to the Post Office and Mr. Bampkin, the Postmaster, asked if he wanted to earn money delivering telegrams. He was paid sixpence per delivery for telegrams to the Camp and one shilling for telegrams further afield. This was at a time when his pocket money was only two pennies a week. When he went back to school he continued to call at the Post Office to earn more money. However, his lucrative income ended when telephones were installed at the Camp.

Security on the main Camp was not very high, and locals were able to use Camp facilities, such as the Cinema, and mess-room bar. Regular weekly dances were held to which local girls were invited, some met their future husbands. One of the village girls remembers meeting her future husband after Church Parade.

Living in Atlantic View was a retired policeman from Leicester whose wife was German. Rumours began of mysterious lights and signalling between Atlantic View and a German submarine in Manorbier Bay, and one of the villagers went to the house with a twelve-bore shotgun to ensure that their loyalties stayed with Britain.

Beaches were protected by scaffolding with barbed wire entanglements and barbed wire on the clifftops. Many items were washed up on shore from ships which had been sunk. One lot of treasure was really appreciated, 45 gallon drums of Aviation spirit, which kept the vehicles running in the Parish for some time. A less happy occurrence was the body of an unidentified airman, washed up on Lydstep Beach, who was buried in St. James Churchyard.

A reliable water supply was needed when the Camp was built. The existing pumping station in Park Farm valley had not been needed when a piped supply had come to the Parish, so it was put back into service for the Camp. This pumping station is still in existence although it has not been used for several years. Italian prisoners of war were employed to lay additional water mains so that a lot of the outlying farms could be connected to a supply, rather than rely on their own wells. Although there was no electricity in the Parish, the Camp obviously required electricity, so this

was laid on by West Cambrian Power Co. Manorbier Church set up a lighting fund in 1940 and were connected by the next year and several other houses in Manorbier were connected later, including Fernley Lodge and Glan-y-Môr.

There were a few places where one could obtain a cup of tea and other refreshments. Mrs. Walters from Whitewell Farm ran a shop and café at Lydstep, now the Lydstep Tavern, and people from the Camp had fond memories of time spent there. They remembered the ham and eggs, which was a rarely seen treat during the war years. Mrs. Walters was helped in the shop by her daughters. One day an RAF officer was passing the farm on his bicycle and he fell off at the bridge under the railway. One of the daughters came out to help him, a romance started and Jack Cowper married Maisie Walters.

The Dak used to do a nicely poached egg on toast, and the lady running the café used to send her husband out to fetch and carry. Having lived in India for many years (hence the name 'Dak' being an Indian word meaning 'Post' or 'transport' by relays of men), he always wore a linen suit and a panama hat, summer or winter. The café had been built on to the original half of the WWI hut, and the window was left in to keep the café separate from the rest of the building.

When the war began, it was decided to form local defence units, which eventually became the Home Guard. One was formed at Manorbier and, in the early days, there

*Soldiers in the Dak Café*

Adams and Albert Watts. The Platoon trained in the Castle, and one of the village boys can remember throwing stones to annoy them. They joined in the Church parades that both the Army and RAF held.

The regular Army were a bit dismissive of the men's help and during a training exercise, one of the Home Guard, who was guarding a bridge, was jumped on by soldiers, who threw him in the water. They then stole the bolt from his gun, which he had to get back from the Army at Lamphey. As the Home Guard became more capable, they were able to beat the Army during exercises, their local knowledge giving them an advantage.

Auxiliary Units were attached to the Home Guard, and were trained in sabotage and to act as a guerrilla force in the event of invasion. The remains of a chamber exists beyond the Dak, overlooking Bramley Cove, which is said to be the remains of the base of an Auxiliary Unit in Manorbier. Unfortunately, there is no documentary proof of this.

The local policeman had to ensure that the blackout regulations were kept. He lived in Penally and his area included Manorbier Parish. He cycled around his patch, which covered the Army camps, and would sometimes find himself having to prevent fights between the various units. There were also Special Constables, whose job was to patrol from Giltar to Swanlake but, according to Home Guard members, they spent most of their time in a hut playing cards.

were no uniforms, rifles, or any other type of equipment. Anyone who had a gun and had some idea how to use it was recruited, young or old. Initially inexperienced (there was a tale that they first marched with loaded shotguns over their shoulders pointing at other members of the Guard), their performance soon became more professional, with Jimmy John as the Officer and Ronnie Williams of Middle Hill Farm as one of the Sergeants. Other members were Teddy Johns, Roly Hughes, Rupert Edwards, Wallace Cater, Harry

# EVACUEES

In the autumn of 1940, several evacuees came to the Parish and were placed at houses and farms around the villages. Some stayed for the duration of the war, and one stayed all his life, taking up farming. Two sisters, Irene and Mae Brown, were aged 13 and 9 when they arrived. They later wrote down their impressions and memories of their time as evacuees. They and their mother stayed at Fernley Lodge, in a flat above the stables. Fernley Lodge was then owned by Mr. and Mrs. Jimmy John. He was farming and his wife had been running the Lodge as a Guest House. Officers from the Camp were billeted on them. The girls, who had come from Lewisham, were used to more modern conveniences than were available in Manorbier. They were surprised that the lighting was by oil lamps, the water had to be fetched from a tap in the yard and the lavatory was outside.

They became friends with the large family of Frank Hughes, the grocer, with Irene becoming friendly with Jean Kitchen (née Hughes) and her sister Gwyneth, and Mae being friends with Ann and Audrey. Irene remembers the butcher at South Norton, Mr. Rogers, hanging moleskins to dry outside his shop.

Mrs. Brown became bored, and she began helping out at Glan-y-Môr and the lodge, preparing food for the officers billeted there. She also found entertainment at the Parish Hall, where every Saturday, a whist drive and dance was held, to which she would take her eldest daughter, Irene. Although she herself did not dance, she would sit by the fire talking to her new friends, as well as keeping an eye on her daughter, who had learnt to dance and was much in demand.

At one of these dances, Irene met Micky, a Cockney and a bright character, who worked for Frank Hughes in the grocer's shop. Micky used to organise concerts for the troops. Hearing that Irene had learned to tap-dance, as had Gwyneth Hughes, he made them both practise and then arranged for them to join one of his concerts at the St. Florence Pilots Training Camp. The land along the Ridgeway had never been ploughed and was non-productive moorland and the girls describe walking over the moors, in the dark, to the concert. When it was their turn, they went through the two numbers that they had rehearsed, accompanied by whistles and shouts from their appreciative audience. Cigarette smoke made a fog in the hall, and their audience had been drinking.

Irene could not remember much after they had finished, but a fight broke out in the audience, and they were jostled and chatted up by the lads as they retreated to the cloakroom, found their coats and set off home, older and wiser. Neither of them ever performed again at a concert. Jean Kitchen also remembers being there that evening without knowing that her sister and friend were part of the night's entertainment. She was mortified to see them on stage tap-dancing to the tune, 'Come get together, let the dance floor feel your leather, etc., etc.'

The first Christmas for the Brown family at Manorbier was notable in that they had a surprise invitation to join the Hughes family for a Christmas party. It was a big jolly party, with lots of noise and activity.

## AGRICULTURE DURING THE WAR

During the war, farming was strictly controlled by the War Agricultural Executive Committee (War Ag) set up for each County, which enabled the Government to control what crops farmers grew, and make sure that farmers sold most of their crops via the government. Meadow and moor land were ploughed up, and this was when the Ridgeway moors began to be cultivated. There were only three tractors in the Parish during the war and the War Ag had tractors of their own, which they let out to farmers for their use. They had a Caterpillar D2 which was strong enough to pull a deep plough to bury the gorse and other plants which formed the moors. At Norchard, they had an International 10-20, which they changed for a more modern track-laying machine, an International T20 which was imported from America.

Both before and during the war, there was a mill at Norchard, the only one in the Parish after the Castle mill had closed in about 1900. Corn was milled there with neighbouring farmers bringing wheat, barley and oats to be ground, some into flour for human consumption, and some to make animal feed. During one harvest time in August 1940, the oil tanks at Llanreath were set on fire, a fire that raged for three weeks. This carried oil into the air, and descended on the sheaves and stooks in the fields, and the harvesters themselves were covered in oil. Threshing machines went from farm to farm, with a gang of men whose job was to set up the machine and make sure it kept going. John 'Nacky' Stephens of Cooper's Lake, Manorbier Newton, was one of the local pioneers for this new type of farm equipment. At Norchard they used their own steam engine, a Robey, but it was not self-propelled, and had to be pulled into position by a team of horses.

Sugar beet became a major crop although the nearest factory was in Shropshire, main crop potatoes were also encouraged. These crops were sent from Manorbier station, as were animals for the Government slaughterhouses. Hay, straw and mangolds were loaded onto railway wagons in the goods yard at the station, and these were sent to the South Wales coal mines to feed the pit ponies. There used to be a height gauge at the end of the platform to make sure that the loaded wagons were not too high to get through the tunnels. Another crop that was sent from the station was rabbit, which was still available in large numbers.

During the winter, sheep, brought down from the Preseli Hills, were fed turnips and hay in the fields. The sheep had to be dipped once a year to prevent the fly, with a police-man being present to witness it, which was often done in the stream below the old mill in Manorbier. When it became warmer, the sheep were sheared, initially by hand shears. Shears were then invented which were driven by turning a handle while the shearer sheared the sheep. Roger Minchin can remember being allowed to turn the handle of these when he was young, and he was always told off for not keeping the shears going, which was hard work for a young boy.

Farm work was made a reserved occupation by the Government at the beginning of the war. As the war went on, more men were needed in the forces. To replace them, the Government had created the Women's Land Army. Land Girls were based at Hodgeston Hill Farm, just outside the parish and some of them were billeted at the farms where they worked. This influx of young women into the parish had quite an effect on the local lads, and some of the Land Girls were quite happy to join in the fun.

One of the local girls, Olive Howells, later Woods, who lived at Spring Hill, joined the Land Army. She remembers that the Land Army girls were invited to dances at the American camp at Lamphey Palace. They went several times, until, after one of the dances, the girls, instead of being taken back, were driven about three miles further, and shoved out to make their own way home. Olive never did find out what they had done wrong. Later, when she was working with one of the Italian prisoners, he suddenly changed completely, and threatened her with a pitchfork. Olive retreated to the farmhouse, and she and the farmer's wife shut the door on him. Eventually, the farmer arrived and the police were called and the prisoner taken away.

The first prisoners of war to arrive in the area were Italians, who had been captured in the Western Desert. Later in the war, German prisoners began to arrive. The Germans were imprisoned at Clynderwen and brought out in trucks to the farms that needed help. There were already people of Italian descent in the area, such as the Fecci family of Tenby. Some of the prisoners became friendly with these local families and stayed on after the war. The Italians built a set of steps down to Skrinkle beach, which is now closed. The most troublesome of the German prisoners had red flashes on their clothes, and worked in small gangs with an armed guard. More trusted men were allowed to stay on the farms, rather than be returned to camp every night. After one of the plane crashes, some prisoners had obtained Perspex from the windshields and used it to make a variety of objects, including rings, necklaces and cigarette lighters, which they sold to the locals. When the war ended, the prisoners were repatriated, and almost all were gone by 1947.

# TRAGEDY OF WAR

There were several aircraft which crashed in the Parish during the war, some from B Flight of No. 1 A.A.C.U. There were three crashes by Hawker Henley aircraft, one in April 1940, when a plane was taking off from Carew Cheriton and the engine cut out on take off and it came down just over the Ridgeway in Manorbier Newton. The second occurred in May 1940, when the pilot accidentally switched off the ignition of the plane during take off from RAF Manorbier and it crashed on the Point to Point field in Lydstep. Both crews were unhurt.

The third crash was in December 1940, when a Polish pilot was performing a 'diving' sortie for the gunnery school. He crashed into the sea at Skrinkle Bay and was killed. Another Polish pilot in July 1941 hit the ground in a turn at Manorbier Camp, flying a Tiger Moth, killing himself and his crew member.

In March 1943 a Bristol Blenheim took off from Carew Cheriton on convoy patrol, developed engine trouble and ditched in the sea 100 yards from the shore at Swanlake Bay. Happily, the crew survived. The final crash happened in October 1943, when a Wellington had engine problems during a ferry flight, and, as it descended, struck the roof of Calvesland Farm, ripping off a wing. The plane crashed in a field the other side of the road, killing both the crew.

Among the young men of the Parish who fought in the Second World War, there were five deaths.

One of the fallen was Austin Johns, who was a stoker on the light cruiser *HMS Neptune*. This ship was part of a group of cruisers and destroyers that struck an Italian minefield off Tripoli in December 1941 and the *Neptune* and one of the destroyers were sunk. Of the 757 men aboard *HMS Neptune*, only one survived.

Joe Kidney, who was also in the Navy, lost his life while serving on the aircraft carrier, *HMS Glorious*, in June 1940. The ship was assisting in the evacuation of British troops from Norway and sailed with two escorting destroyers. They were attacked by two German battle cruisers, *Scharnhorst* and *Gneisenau*, and all three British ships were sunk, with only 39 survivors. There was an official enquiry later as to why the aircraft carrier had sailed with such a small escort.

Benjamin Warlow died in a Japanese prisoner of war camp at Macassar on the island of Celebes on the 19th of April 1945, just before the Japanese surrender. He had been in the Navy on *HMS Repulse* when it was sunk by Japanese bombers in December 1941. He survived and then joined the destroyer *HMS Encounter*. At the battle of the Java Seas this ship was also sunk on the 1st March 1942. Again he survived, but was captured by the Japanese and died three years later.

Morgan Williams of Manorbier, was a corporal in the 1/5th Battalion, Welch Regiment. The Battalion was sent to Normandy in late June 1944 as reinforcements for the D-day Beachhead. After Montgomery's attack to the east of Caen from 17th to 20th of July, the German forces attempted to retrieve some of the ground lost with a counter-attack on 21st July. The Battalion held them off after hours of desperate fighting, but Morgan Williams was one of the men killed on that day.

John Adams, who had been born in Manorbier, was in the Merchant Navy when the War began. He was in convoys that plied between the U.K. and the U.S.A. His ship, *M.V. Oakcrest*, was torpedoed in the Atlantic on 2nd December 1940. He was one of the few crew to reach a lifeboat, which drifted for twelve days before being washed up on the Isle of Barra in the Outer Hebrides. Several of these men died but John was lucky. He then joined the R.N.R. and was serving on *H.M.T. Stella Capella*, on anti-submarine duty, when it was lost south of Iceland on 19th March 1942. No one survived.

# AFTER THE SECOND WORLD WAR

There was a general shortage of housing after the war and houses with a projected life of only ten years were designed for factory production. One type of these factory-made homes was called the Airey house, which was made of pre-cast columns and walls. Eight of these semi-detached homes (four blocks) were built at Bush Terrace in Jameston, and they are still there today, more than sixty years later.

According to the authors of *Pevsner Guide to the Buildings of Pembrokeshire*, Jameston was "once one of South Pembrokeshire's best preserved villages. Several cottages had round or square chimneys of the sixteenth century, all surviving until shortly after the Second World War, when local authority housing was built and the main road straightened." For the residents of the cottages, the reality was different. Some of the houses had no water or electricity, and those in the centre of the village had no gardens, which meant that there was no room for an earth closet. People had to walk as far as two hundred yards to find an earth closet which was shared between several cottages. As they were unfit for habitation, the occupants were re-housed in the Airey houses and the cottages demolished, to be replaced by twenty properties in St. James Place.

There were only forty houses in the village of Manorbier after the war. There were plans to rapidly increase the size of Manorbier, but this did not meet with approval and the scheme was dropped. A smaller estate of twelve properties was built in Manor Crescent.

A new development of seven bungalows and one house was built in Pembroke Road, Manorbier, in 1963, just in time for the completion of the Regent (now Valero) refinery at Rhoscrowther. Most of these new houses were purchased by people working at the refinery, and they became known as 'Oily Row'. Further houses were built in Warlows Close in Manorbier, when ten properties were constructed. The Close was extended in 1973 when sixteen properties were added, and the road was renamed Warlows Meadow. There was a problem in extending this site, due to a large rock outcrop, which prevented any further building. According to the story, the problem was solved by the builder meeting an Irishman in a pub in Pembroke Dock, who claimed to be an expert with explosives. This man was employed, and he successfully blasted away the crag, but unfortunately a rain of rock fragments fell on the village, damaging several cars, including a much prized vintage motor car.

Lydstep has increased in size, with some in-filling, and a small estate built on the west side of the village.

Manorbier Newton has also spread, with in-filling in fields along Cowpark Lane.

Manorbier had a new sewerage system and sewage treatment works built in 1953 and Jameston was eventually connected to the new works ten years later and the old cesspit abandoned. After treatment, the outfall for the effluent was in the Bay.

There was a scheme in 1973 to build an outfall right out into the middle of Manorbier Bay to take sewage from the whole of the South Pembrokeshire area, and experiments were carried out which apparently proved that all of the sewage would be taken out to sea. The villagers objected to this plan and a tremendous legal battle ensued with the villagers being victorious, and the plan was abandoned. Eventually a new works was built at Gumfreston in the late nineties. A pumping main from Manorbier was laid to the new works at Gumfreston, and the Manorbier works became a storm overflow.

When the war ended, the restrictions on crops that the farmers were allowed to grow were removed, and one of the first crops to be revived were early potatoes. Most of local new potato growing ended in the eighties, when supermarkets began to import from Egypt. Potatoes began to be grown under plastic everywhere, which negated any advantage that Pembrokeshire had.

*The bulb factory, Manorbier Newton, with two large greenhouses and packing buildings*

An unusual crop for the Parish was tulips and daffodils. They were grown by the Van Geest company, for the bulbs, on fields towards the Ridgeway. Their bulb factory was in Manorbier Newton, with two large greenhouses and packing buildings.

Mr. Van Geest built three prefabricated bungalows in Manorbier Newton for his employees.

One was lived in by his secretary, and the second by Mr. and Mrs. Day. He drove tractors for the company and his wife also sometimes worked for them. The third prefab was lived in by Dennis Lewis, who was a bricklayer originally from Liverpool. Mr. Lewis erected the prefabs, and also built the greenhouses and the other buildings. Mr. Day's father-in-law, Mr. Brown lived at Fern Hill, and was the general foreman.

After the war, the secret establishment at Lydstep was closed and moved to Aberporth. The School of Artillery continued, and heavy automatic guns using radar for tracking were installed at the firing range. It was realised that the air threat of the Cold War was changing defence systems and heavy guns were unable to bring down enemy planes. They were replaced by *Thunderbird Mk. 1* surface to air missiles, and a special security compound was built for them in 1958, at Skrinkle headland. The *Thunderbird Mk. 1* entered service with the Royal Artillery in 1959. The *Thunderbird Mk. 2* missile system followed in 1964.

The Army built married quarters on the runways of the RAF station and the station buildings were demolished, apart from the Officer's Mess, which was used as a medical centre. The four roads in the estate were named after the first four Commandants of the School of Artillery, namely Wheeler, Hounsell, Gray and Dewing. There were between five and six hundred Army personnel based at Manorbier which provided a lot of employment within the area. Unfor-

tunately, by 1970, savings were required, and finally on 1st April 1972, the Camp was closed.

In its thirty-six years Manorbier School of Artillery made a vital contribution to the country's defence during both the Second World War and the Cold War.

Owing to the excellent facilities available at Manorbier, the Army decided to retain it as a Firing Range, and the Royal Artillery Range, Manorbier, was formed in 1972. Under the command of Castlemartin Range it is still used by units of the Marines, the Regular Army and the Territorial Army, to practise firing the *Starstreak* missiles currently in use.

The housing for Officers and N.C.O.'s at Skrinkle, built by the Birmingham firm of Dudley Boswell in the early sixties, was released by the Ministry of Defence in 1978. The twenty or so houses for Officers were sold, and the remaining 94 were initially retained by the County Council, although the majority are now privately owned. Skrinkle is now a thriving community and almost a separate village in its own right. The Skrinkle Community Hall, rented from the Youth Hostel Association, holds many local events and has established clubs for various organisations. The YHA Hostel and the Community Hall was formerly the instructional building for the *Thunderbird* surface to air missile when it was being developed at the School of Gunnery.

Lydstep House had been purchased by Mr. Harry Thomas. It became a guest house and Mr. Thomas allowed campers and pioneer caravanners to stay on the land overlooking Lydstep Bay. Motor and motorcycle hill climbs were staged in the early fifties from in front of the house towards the North Lodge. As the number of caravanners increased, space was set aside for static caravans, which were becoming popular. Eventually the whole of the site was used for static caravans. David Thomas, Harry's son, eventually sold the caravan park to Pontins in 1982 and it is now owned by Bourne Leisure.

A group in Lydstep recently attempted to obtain funding for restoring the Palace for use as a village hall, craft workshop and shop. Unfortunately, they did not succeed, partly because they could not convince funders that the proposals were viable, and also because there were no parking spaces available. The Palace was made safe by the Park Authority; no public access is allowed and it is beginning to deteriorate again.

Tourism was becoming a major industry in Pembrokeshire. Castle Mead, in Manorbier, became a hotel in the early sixties run by Mr. Peter Davie. Glan-y-Môr, which had reverted to a hotel after the war, had a restaurant for customers and non-residents. The hotel changed hands in 1964 and the new owners decided that they would increase the size of their dining area, and add three bars to the front of the building, creating a new pub called the Pirates Lantern, and a tea-room was opened at The Lodge. During the sixties and early seventies, the hotels were fully booked, and

there was lots of trade for the pubs and hotels. Both the Castle Inn and Pirates Lantern had large car parks, and they were so busy during the season, that a car park attendant had to be employed.

The Pembrokeshire Coast National Park Authority was formed in 1952 and is the only Coastal National Park in the United Kingdom. One of the first things that the Authority did was to prevent the extraction of sand from the beach in 1953, so they purchased the sand extraction firms. There had been a caravan site on the beach after the war, but the lease from the Picton Estate ended. The Park decided to build a car park on the former caravan site in 1967 and purchased the land. Car park walls were built, a footpath laid down to the beach, and lavatories erected on the site of the old Mill House. The Park told the owners of Tranquillity, the hut above Manorbier Bay that it had either to be repaired or demolished, and the owners decided to demolish it. The area in front was improved and resurfaced to accommodate about twenty cars for short-term parking.

The Manorbier Women's Institute was formed in 1965. The following year they held a Variety Nite in the Parish Hall which was a great success. They played a football match against Manorbier cricket team, and won by seven goals to three. According to a report of the match, the ladies were at times helped by the enthusiastic spectators.

*Manorbier W.I. Football Team, 1967*
*Standing (from left): Margaret Williams, Val Bolter, Margaret Lewis, Joan John, Janet Francis, Rhona Francis, Joyce Kidney, Queenie Williams.*
*Kneeling: Jo Stern, Jean Vincent, Betty Thomas*

Manorbier W.I. entered a 'Harassed House-wives' sketch at the Group Spring Council meeting in 1976 at the Torch Theatre, and finished second, although according to some non-biased observers, they should have finished first.

Every year they held Senior Citizens Christmas Parties, with entertainment provided by members, including Gwen Rothwell, who was older than most of the 'Senior Citizens' there. At the first visit of the twinned town of Vernau in France in 1986, the ladies of the W.I. provided tea in the Castle.

Some friendly matches of cricket and football had been played during the War, but the leagues soon started again. Football was played on a pitch on the old RAF camp at Manorbier, and this is the pitch still in use.

Cricket also began again, and a pavilion was built on a leased field in Manorbier, for both football and cricket players. Unfortunately, the cricket team has been disbanded.

The Army had their own sports field on the Camp. They had a cricket team that played matches all over Wales, and even had Glamorgan County team visit to play a match. The captain of the Army team was a Sri Lankan Colonel, who was jailed on his return home

1961

*Standing (left to right): Gordon Roblin, Philip Johns, Keith Scourfield, Bertie Johns, Ashley Skyrme, Kenny Warlow, Ralph Johns, Gerald Thomas.*
*Seated: Billy Phillips, Harry Cater, Glyn Rixon, Trevor Howells, Wynford Phillips*

for involvement in a conspiracy to overthrow the government. During the winter, the Army played Rugby, and their team was very successful.

# PARISH PEOPLE

John Garfield Davies, who had become Vicar of St. James Church in 1937, was the last of the churchmen to live in the Victorian Vicarage. He was the first vicar who had not been appointed by Christ's College, Cambridge, who had held that privilege since 1508. An Oxford graduate, he was the author of the booklet still for sale in St. James Church today, *Manorbier Church and Parish*. John Garfield Davies was appointed Canon of St. Davids Cathedral in 1957. He and his wife ran the Sunday School although the school outings did not re-start after the war. One of the children from Jameston recalls that after Sunday School, they were invited for tea at the Vicarage and the children were allowed to run up one set of stairs, and down the other. This, for children who lived in cottages without stairs, was the height of adventure. Afterwards they would walk home to Jameston, via Atlantic View, where they would be given chocolate cornflake cakes by Mrs. Brown. It was said that John Garfield Davies "loved the Lord and the Lord's women."

The present vicarage was built for the new vicar, Rev. Robert Williams, when he came to the Parish in 1963. He and his wife were much liked. He occasionally played the organ in St. James, and sometimes preached at Penuel Baptist Church. A keen swimmer, he participated in the Boxing Day swim at Tenby. He used the water from the spring at Shute Cottage to brew his home-made beer, insisting that no other water was as good. There is a tale that he was caught drink driving, and blamed it on the fact that he had had to finish off the communion wine. Banned from driving, he visited his parishioners riding a bicycle. Gwen Rothwell's husband Jim was good friends with the Vicar, and they would spend many evenings drinking together. According to Gwen, they were as bad as each other. He retired in 1983.

Every Christmas Eve, the children went carol singing, and knew which of the houses were more generous and where silver, rather than copper, was given to the collectors. There was also a tradition for carol singing on New Year's Day but only before noon. They started in Manorbier, went around the villages, and finished in Lamphey at the Bakers where they treated themselves to cakes, before catching the train home.

Glyn Rixon remembers helping Mr. Rogers, the butcher at South Norton, to deliver trays of meat to customers in his van. When the Jameston children were sent to pick up the family meat from Mr. Rogers, they would then walk along the Castle footpath (no longer in use) to pick up groceries at Mr. Frank Hughes' shop and then back to Jameston via Park Valley.

Dennis 'The Shop' Williams and his wife, Maggie, took over the grocer's shop in Jameston from his parents. He had joined the Fleet Air Arm in 1941, and after the War worked at De Havilland on the new jet airliner, the Comet, until he returned to Jameston when his parents retired in 1962.

Miss Hilda Thomas bought her first Sealyham dog when she was ten years old in 1901 when her parents were living at the Grange. She bought her first bitch in 1912, which cost her 30s.0d. She had to save up for her, which she did by trapping moles, skinning them, and selling them to a dealer in Bristol for 2d each. She then took the bitch to mate, paid the fee, and promised the owner of the stud dog the pick of the litter. Unfortunately, her bitch only had one pup, so Hilda finished with nothing. Fortunately, the second try gave a large litter, and from there she became a very successful breeder and did well in shows, having twelve Champions in the thirties. She married late in life, becoming Mrs. Hilda Lloyd, and moved next door to Baldwins Moor. She continued to breed and show her dogs until the 1980's.

The Brace family lived and worked at the Beaver's Hill railway crossing for many years, until their retirement when they moved into Jameston. Their replacement, Dai the engine, was relaxing in the Swan Lake Inn one day and

lost track of the time. He ran and was almost at the crossing when the train went through the gates. They were demolished, and had to be rebuilt. The unlucky keeper had it happen to him again soon after, so he tried a different job.

The gatekeeper at Manorbier Newton crossing, Mrs. Beddoes, knocked one of the village boys off his bicycle. She was more concerned about her gates than him or his bike, so to take revenge, the boys used her well as a urinal. Some of them used to hang on to the cantilevered end of the signal so that the poor woman could hardly move it. There is another side to the story, as she had been mercilessly teased by the children going back and forth across the Railway line, shouting "Gate" to her every time they wanted to go across. She got upset about this, and asked the mothers to try and stop their children annoying her. Despite all this, she lived until she was almost one hundred years old. After the Beeching Report of 1963 on the railways, both of the Halts were closed, the crossing gates removed and the cottages at the crossings knocked down. There is now no warning of an approaching train, although there are warning lights at Manorbier Station crossing.

Just before the end of the war, the Dak café had been bought by two men, Albert Walters and his friend, who was nicknamed Happy Jim. They stayed there for a few years until a Mr. and Mrs. Atkinson purchased the property. They continued to run it as a café and bed and breakfast, until about 1972. There was, by then a piped water supply from a

spring on the hill towards Atlantic View. The spring was fenced off from cattle but they occasionally broke down the fence. When the occupants of the Dak noticed their water becoming a strange green colour, they knew that the cattle had broken the fence again. A mains supply of water was eventually laid in the 90's. The café has been closed, but part of it is still used as holiday accommodation.

After the war, the newly-married Jack Cowper continued to fly with civil airlines and he was one of the first pilots for BOAC. Lord Louis Mountbatten was flown back to Britain after the partition of India in 1947 and Jack Cowper was his pilot. When he left the airline he took up a new life as a partner in a building company and built a house and shop at Lydstep, which his wife Maisie ran, opposite her mother's original shop. When the shop closed, it became a private house and the car park was sold to the Lydstep Tavern.

Ivor Mathias had married Winifred Lewis in 1930. After he died the Norchard farm was run by his two sons, Fred, and George. Like his father, who was a leading amateur Point to Point rider, Fred also achieved success as a jockey and rode 89 winners, his best known horse being called Lydstep Haven. The family started the Lydstep Point to Point meetings, still held every Easter.

Another of Fred's claims to fame was an episode that occurred after a loss by Wales in a rugby international against England at Twickenham, in 1958. Terry Davies, the Wales

*Fred Mathias*
(By kind permission of Diana Mathias and Squibb's Studio, Tenby)

full back, hit the crossbar during an attempt at goal, and, if it had gone over, Wales would have won. During the commiserations afterwards, someone suggested that the offending crossbar should be removed. So Fred and his friends went to Diana's (shortly to become his wife) nearby home, to borrow a saw. Fred climbed up the post and unhooked the heavy crossbar with some difficulty and it came down with an almighty crash. Fortunately no one heard, and they sawed off the end three feet. They tied a large leek to the goal post as their calling card. The culprits divided the

crossbar into three equal pieces. The next day on the way home they stopped at a café where they found Terry Davies and he signed the piece of crossbar for Fred. Fortunately, the Rugby Union saw the funny side of it, forgave them and did not press charges.

Gerald and Betty Thomas were the children of Frederick Thomas who was wounded in the First World War and who died in December 1919. His wife, who was an assistant schoolteacher at the school, brought up her two children on her own. They lived in Carew Cottage, next to Beach Break, and their house was used as the Doctor's surgery when he came on his weekly visit to the village. Gerald, nicknamed 'Hobbs' after the famous Jack Hobbs, was a very keen cricketer (he always entered a room swiping an imaginary bat stroke). He kept wicket in the Manorbier team for many years. His sister Betty was very active in the W.I. and the Red Cross and she looked after several of the elderly people in Manorbier. After her death from cancer in 1970, a collection was organised, and a new clock bought and placed on the Parish Hall, together with a plaque, in her memory. The inscription reads "This clock was given in memory of Betty Thomas 1919-70 whose unselfish work in the Parish endeared her to the people of Manorbier."

Wilfred Hicks, the singer who we met earlier performing in the Parish Hall, was a builder and stonemason. He had been born in Carew and was apprenticed to a local builder. He was one of a large family, and although he won a scholar-ship to Grammar school, his parents could not afford to send him and he started his apprenticeship at the age of thirteen. Some years after being trained, he went into partnership, and the partners worked on several of the large houses in the area, including Cresselly House and Upton Castle. One day, he unfortunately got some lime mortar in his eye, which was very painful. He went to the doctors to be treated, and it was a bit better, but not much. Then he remembered working with an old chap who had had the same problem and whose wife had cured it. He went to see her and she told him to find a snail, jab it, then squeeze the snail juice into his eye. This rather gruesome method was successful.

Mr. Hicks and his partner built many of the stone walls that can still be seen in several villages in the area. He was an expert on the Latin names of all plants. A Jameston man can remember being in the garden of a house talking to the householders about their beans, when a voice from above informed them of the correct Latin names. It was Wilfred Hicks, working on the roof. He built the altar in the Memorial Chapel in the Church when the North transept was changed in 1964.

Roly Hughes, the eldest son of Frank Hughes, farmed at Hill Farm. He was a member of the Home Guard. Although ammunition was short at the beginning of the War, Roly decided to practise his rifle shooting. A house in the village had a swivelling metal cowl on the chimney, and it was a

good target, as you could see if there had been a hit. The householder was none too pleased, but did not find the culprit. Another time, after the war, he was playing in a cricket match, and complained so long about the Umpire's decision, that the Umpire threw him off the pitch. "You can't do that," says Roly Hughes, "this is my field." Unfortunately, his argument did not impress the Umpire, who banished him from the pitch and throughout the rest of the match, Roly could be seen peeping over the field hedge. When he was much older, he was visiting the Doctor, and an acquaintance saw him and asked him how he was. After some general conversation, Roly came out with the startling idea that he wanted to die by being shot. This naturally amazed his enquirer, but Roly wanted to be shot by a very jealous husband. This was when he was in his eighties.

# THE PICTON ESTATE TODAY

The Picton Estate still own land in the Parish but not as much as they originally had. The Estate had about a fifth of the acreage of the Parish when they obtained it from Thomas Bowen and they continued to have this amount until the effects of Death Duty, which started in 1894, began to be felt. Sir Richard Philipps was created Baron Milford in 1776 but this title became extinct when he died childless in 1823. In his Will, Lord Milford left the Estate to a distant relative who changed his name to Philipps, and the Baronetcy passed to the grandfather of Lord St. David's of Lydstep House.

The Estate stayed in the hands of the Philipps family until the 1930's when Sheila Philipps married Baron de Rutzen of Slebech in 1932. Her husband, who was serving in the Welsh Guards, was killed in Italy in 1944. Sheila de Rutzen re-married Lt. Colonel Randal Plunkett in 1947, who on his father's death, became Lord Dunsany with Sheila becoming Lady Dunsany. Her brother Johnny was found dead in his bath in 1949 so Sheila inherited the Picton Estate from him. There was a daughter from her first marriage, Victoria, who married Sir Francis Dashwood and they had three daughters, Emily, Caroline and Gina. Sheila, Lady Dunsany, had another daughter from her second marriage, the Hon. Beatrice Plunkett. Lady Dunsany disposed of Picton Castle to another branch of the Philipps family. Rumour has it she said that as she and her husband already had twenty-seven castles one less would not really matter.

Lady Dunsany lived most of her life at Dunsany Castle in County Meath. When she died in 1999, her obituary said: "Lady Dunsany remained a beautiful woman into old age, retaining her trim and elegant figure." Miss Beatrice Plunkett has inherited the remnants of the Estate, which now consists of the Parish Hall, a farm and a few houses in the Parish. The Castle is owned by a family company.

# THE PARISH TODAY

After over one thousand years of recorded history, the Parish of Manorbier has changed dramatically. No longer a Barony of the de Barri's, with hardly any of the Parish in the hands of their successors, the Picton Estate, most of the agricultural land is owned by the farmers who work it. There are over six hundred houses in the Parish with the majority privately owned and the remainder split between rented accommodation, both private and Council, with some second homes and holiday accommodation.

There are no tailors, shoemakers, bakers, millers, or wheelwrights but there are still farmers, builders, gardeners and plasterers. There are new occupations which would never have been dreamt of by the inhabitants many years ago, such as electricians, plumbers, and Refinery workers. Manorbier and Lydstep have Garden Centres and overlooking Lydstep Bay there is a holiday complex with Golf Course and a Spa, Celtic Haven.

The Parish still has three Public Houses, the Lydstep Tavern, the Swanlake Inn and the Castle Inn at Manorbier. The Tudor Lodge has now become a public house. The Mission Hall in Jameston, after a lot of fund-raising and effort by Jameston residents, has been opened this year (2012) as the Village Hall. It now has a large extension at the rear with a kitchen, utilities and a car park. Manorbier Parish Hall, leased from the Picton Estate, is still used for parties, bazaars and fetes. Throughout the summer the Country Market opens once a week to tempt everyone with their display of crafts and plants, cakes and jams. The garage started by Teddy Johns still exists on its original site opposite the Castle Inn. There are two general stores, one at Jameston and one at Manorbier with a Post Office. There is one hotel, the Castle Mead at Manorbier. On the site of Frank Hughes' former store is Beach Break Tea Room which also has a Surf and Beach Shop and a Gift Shop. The owners of Lydstep Farm, just outside the Parish, diversified into a large gardening company. Daffodils are being grown again at Springfields who also provide the county and beyond with delicious asparagus and strawberries in the summer months.

Manorbier Castle is a popular tourist destination as is St. James Church itself with visitors from all over the world signing the visitors book. The Beach is widely regarded as one of the best Surfing venues and even during the winter the sea is often full of wetsuited figures bobbing and riding in the waves.

The Parish has several Camping and Caravan sites, with the majority at Manorbier and a few at Jameston. Several houses offer Bed and Breakfast accommodation.

The composition of the population has also changed, with a large number of 'incomers', some working but the majority are retired.

The villages also have, as in the past, their artists, authors and musicians.

Modern restoration work on the Church commenced in 2000 with the roofs repaired, and the tower coated in lime plaster and lime-washed. Improved heating and lighting have been installed, and a kitchen and disabled toilet fitted at the west end of the Church. The Architect is Bartosch & Stokes, and the work is still continuing. It is hoped that the bells and church clock will be working again in time for New Year 2013.

The Church of St. James the Great still overlooks the Castle and sea and we have a Vicar who lives in the new Vicarage. The Vicar ministers to Redberth and St. Florence Churches as well as our own Church. For the first time in St. James' long history the incumbent is a woman, the Rev. Shirley Rayner.

No-one can foresee what will happen to the Parish of Manorbier in the future, but many things will change again.

# BIBLIOGRAPHY

*The Book of South Wales, the Wye and Coast*, Mr. and Mrs. S. C. Hall.

*The Buildings of Wales: Pembrokeshire*, Tom Lloyd, Julian Orbach, Robert Scourfield.

*The Civil War in Pembrokeshire*, Terry John.

*The Girls behind the Guns*, Dorothy Brewer Kerr.

*Historic Pembrokeshire Homes and their Families*, Francis Jones.

*A Historical Tour through Pembrokeshire*, Richard Fenton.

*The History of Little England beyond Wales*, Edward Laws.

*A History of Wales*, John Davies

*Introduction to British Prehistory*, J. V. S. Megaw and D. D. A. Simpson.

*The Journey through Wales,* Gerald of Wales. Translated by Lewis Thorpe.

*Manorbere and its Neighbourhood.* "A Tourist".

*The Manor of Manorbier in the early Seventeenth Century*, Robert Walker.

*Manorbier Castle, Pembrokeshire*, D. J. Cathcart King and J. Clifford Perks.

*Manorbier Church and Parish*, J. Garfield Davies.

*The Manorbier Court Rolls and Trefloyne Rentals*, Robert Walker.

*The Meyricks of Bush*, Michael McGarvie.

*More Pembrokeshire Folk Tales*, Brian John.

*On the Architectural Antiquities of South Pembrokeshire*, E. A. Freeman.

*Open fields and farmsteads in Pembrokeshire*, Brian Howells.

*Pembrokeshire County History*, Vol. II, III and IV. General Editors: Elwyn Davies and Brian Howells.

*Place Names of Pembrokeshire*, B. G. Charles.

*Pubs of Pembroke, Tenby and South West Pembrokeshire*, Keith Johnson.

*The Pembroke and Tenby Railway*, M. R. Connop Price.

*Roman and Early Medieval Wales*, Christopher Arnold and Jeffrey Davies.

*Wales in the early Middle Ages*, Wendy Davies.